Severe Autism, Denied Support

Struggling to Survive in the Mainstream

Wrong city!

Wrong era!

Wrong upbringing!

Wrong neurology!

Marla Comm: A troubled life --

--Written by Leonard Jayson

Praise for
"Severe Autism, Denied Support"

Congratulations for a book loaded with interest and difficult to put down.

In her biographical account, Marla Comm is a woman afflicted with autism and co-morbid disorders. There has been a perpetual disconnect, all her life, with extremely sociable parents always appalled by her coldness for people and preference for solitude.

With rare candor virtually nothing in her life is held back, the book is sure to rivet the reader's attention.

In addition, the text gives us a dual advantage: we experience an autistic woman consumed with dysfunctional behavior; the very same individual who, in the next breath, can easily discuss with professional expertise the nuances of her mental disorders.

As a thought provoking service, gleaned from the text, it is suggested that anyone in contact with autistic individuals refrain from the sixteen mistakes alluded to in the final chapter.

"Severe Autism, Denied Support" is a superb read not only for therapists and clinicians, but for parents and teachers - everyone seeking a deeper understanding of autism and co-existing dysfunctions.

---Stanley D. Burton, M.D., Beverly Hills, CA

Certified Member of the American Board of the A.M.A., since 1946, (now retired).

I am thoroughly enjoying this book. . . . Bravo! *"Severe Autism - Denied Support,"* is a monumental work.

While reading Marla's life story, I have laughed and cried. . . .

Thank you for a splendid job in bringing her world to print.

Growing up in a family seeking treatment and answers for my severely autistic sister, *why her?;* I could feel pain and compassion for Marla's isolation from society. Not unlike this wonderful volume, we need additional, accurate accounts; these would provide greater understanding and support for the ever increasing numbers of autistics in our society.

--Dr. Leslynn Catlett, O.D.

Severe Autism, Denied Support

Struggling to Survive in the Mainstream

Condemned by the disorders of her neurology,
Marla lives in a world that is foreign to her.

Note for Librarians: A cataloguing record for this book is available from Library and Archives
Canada at www.collectionscanada.ca/amicus/index-e.html
ISBN 1-4251-1621-3

Printed in Victoria, BC, Canada. Printed on paper with minimum 30% recycled fibre.
Trafford's print shop runs on "green energy" from solar, wind and other environmentally-friendly power sources.

Offices in Canada, USA, Ireland and UK

Book sales for North America and international:
Trafford Publishing, 6E–2333 Government St.,
Victoria, BC V8T 4P4 CANADA
phone 250 383 6864 (toll-free 1 888 232 4444)
fax 250 383 6804; email to orders@trafford.com
Book sales in Europe:
Trafford Publishing (UK) Limited, 9 Park End Street, 2nd Floor
Oxford, UK OX1 1HH UNITED KINGDOM
phone +44 (0)1865 722 113 (local rate 0845 230 9601)
facsimile +44 (0)1865 722 868; info.uk@trafford.com
Order online at:
trafford.com/07-0030

10 9 8 7 6 5 4 3

Acknowledgements

I am indebted to many people for their cooperation and gener-
ous assistance in the preparation of this volume. It is my great
pleasure to acknowledge each of them. Thanks go out to Dr.
Stan Burton, my brother-in-law, Dr. Leslynn Catlett, my op-
tometrist, and Susan J. Moreno, director of MAAP, for their
encouragement and contemplative advice. Arthur Bolton, a
friend, carefully reviewed each chapter and offered numerous
suggestions. Charlotte, my wife, provided some topical refer-
ences for inclusion in the text. She and Chris Harter, my step-
sister, strengthened the project with their wise counsel. During years of my decision making, David Zia, a close friend,
offered insightful advice.

Kudos go to Marla Comm for sharing four of her poems that
enhance the book; and I'm most appreciative that she never
failed to answer my "zillion" questions with clarity and frank
candor.

Finally, Dave Duprey and James Gibson, Trafford Publisher
consultants, have been knowledgeable and supportive.

Book cover design is by Wendy Hoag, superb graphic designer.

Contents

(Throughout the text, words and names with an asterisk, also underlined, are in the glossary.)

FOREWORD
Marla Comm

If' you want to read the heartwarming story of an endearing hero, you won't find it here. If you're looking for a success story with a happy ending, you won't find it here. What you will encounter is the cold truth of a culture that could not accommodate or reconcile itself to a person with severe autism. I am that woman who's about to share her life with you.

These pages do not glow with the stunning achievements that other autistics so proudly write about. Although my life pales in comparison to the full and productive lives of others, it does stand out in *other ways*. When reading the book, you may wonder how many autistic people have had an emotionally abusive upbringing, endured multiple <u>co-morbid</u>* disorders, suffered from hard times, got little or no support, and were forced to live in a wretched environment. Rest assured, not many!

While my story isn't the most inspiring one, it must be told for important reasons. The media focuses only on the most successful autistics and gives the wrong impression that people who have the disorder, but with good IQ's, become gifted super-heroes. It unjustly ignores the plight of countless autistic adults who don't make healthy adjustments and lead marginal lives - like me. By telling my story, I hope to remind the reader that not all high IQ adults do as well as people like <u>Temple Grandin</u>*, and that many of us require lifelong support.

If you work with autistics that have poor language skills, my story will help you better understand their behavior and feelings. My experiences may also serve as lessons to those who are parents of newly diagnosed children and are thinking of mainstreaming them. There's a right way and wrong way to go about it. As my story soon illustrates, you can't just throw the child into regular schooling and expect him to function without individual support. Also true, when he reaches adulthood, support tailored to his special needs is essential - perhaps for his entire life. Some of you may wonder whether mainstreaming was right for me, be it in public school or living on my own as an adult, this book should help you decide.

If you are a mental health professional, my story may enlighten you as to the services required by severely affected autistic adults who attempt to function independently in the community. It will also help you realize the commendable differences that *proper support* and the *right environment* can have in a disabled person's life. I fault those in mental health who refuse to address the problems clients have with their day-to-day *living situations* and also fail to include environmental stress reduction in their treatment plans.

In my desperate search for support and understanding, I contacted countless mental health experts and organizations either to be ignored or not given appropriate advice.

My experiences with Internet list groups and forums were equally disappointing, as were those I had with magazine staff and website owners. While kind enough to publish my correspondence, they offered little else. Despite the importance of my story, it was most difficult finding anyone with a bona fide interest. That was until I met Len Jayson.

While searching the Web, in his quest for knowledge about his own personality differences, Len happened upon one of my online autism letters, in late 1998. On reading it, he took a genuine interest in my plight and responded by e-mail. That early exchange blossomed into a loyal correspondence that still continues to flourish; he has a deeper understanding than people who've known me over four decades! Based on his acceptance of me and my trust in him, I've shared secrets that I dared not tell anyone!

In our e-mail correspondence, as he watched me struggle through each day with burnout and bad living conditions - he knew that mine was a story that needed to be told. He then set about the laborious task of turning reams of e-mail into a compelling biographical story; one that we hope will benefit autistic individuals, also struggling to cope with life in the mainstream.

INTRODUCTION

Leonard Jayson

Making contact with Marla Comm, eight years ago, was a stroke of luck. In researching autism on the Internet, I came across Marla's essay "Barely Making it in the Community." Fascinated by her story, I contacted her and we began an in-depth e-mail correspondence that has never faltered.

The 18th century, English novelist Laurence Sterne once exclaimed: "Writing is but another name for conversation."

Despite living thousands of miles apart, I've had a conversation from "inside" the mind of a multi-dimensional person willing to illuminate her many traits. Marla's degree of openness is unusual for an adult with autism. With high intellect and candor, she has made her neurological disorders understandable. Throughout the book, they are mostly discussed in the context of her current life-situation.

Though my own autism is less severe than Marla's, it has helped me better understand her difficulties. Although I have three additional neurological disorders, she is burdened with many.

Since we've been communicating back-and-forth, there have been over a thousand e-mails - informal letter writing and the source material for this book. Each e-mail jumps around with segments on countless different topics. However, for writing a published book, the text needed editing in terms of structure, style, readability, and grammar.

Marla has the high intelligence to develop unusual insight into her condition and be willing to share it with others. Whenever I got stuck, she always came through with a fast turnaround that would clarify any aspect of her life not understood

Marla was originally against the idea of a book; she believed that when the story is about a person with a dysfunctional life, the reader always anticipates a happy ending. Since the 1990's, Marla's condition has gotten worse instead of better; therefore, she was concerned there'd be no interest in her story.

While not disagreeing with the general viewpoint, I believe that her story is unique and compelling, so that it needs to be told, regardless of book circulation.

To serve the public with realism, it is necessary that the media provide enlightenment as to the nature of autism and other brain disorders; no longer should the media disseminate only success stories but begin to make known more realistic, psychiatric conditions - even those *without* happy endings.

We are advocating improvements on behalf of neurologically and developmentally disabled people; those attempting to lead independent lives and survive in the mainstream. Clients should no longer be denied supportive psychotherapy. The need is for verbal counseling, face-to-face, perhaps weekly sessions, and based on each client's individual circumstances and difficulties.

For convenience, words and names that may be unfamiliar appear in the Glossary. In the text, each one is underlined and has a single asterisk.

Specific text is cross referenced, alerting the reader to a chapter that more fully deals with it.

Because of overlapping, it was necessary to place a few of the chapters somewhat out of sequence.

Your thoughts about the book will be appreciated.

Please send correspondence to:
LJayson@aol.com
marlacomm@hotmail.com

Note: Dr. Webster, psychiatrist, is a pseudonym.

<u>NOTE</u>:

The text I've written is based on Marla Comm's biographical material; the product of our e-mail correspondence. I've endeavored to use a writing style in the Text which puts Marla in the first person - very much human - as though she is talking to the reader.

Marla supplied me with countless anecdotes of her life story in addition to a wide breadth of psychiatric knowledge that never stops growing. Her unique level of understanding is predicated on:

**High intelligence;

**Copious psychiatric and neurological reading;
(done in bits-and-pieces, yet retained by a vivid memory)

**Researching her multiple disoders on the Internet;

**E-mail correspondence and learning from others having similar disorders;

**A deep interest in studying how singly and in synergy each dysfunction has affected her life.

--Leonard Jayson

1

Childhood and Teen Years

INTRODUCTION:
At age 3 and 3 months, due to Marla's lack of speech, she was taken by her parents to see Dr. Hunt, a child psychiatrist, for an evaluation at his neurological clinic.

She was diagnosed as having Autism but with intellectual potential. This evaluation appeared in the clinic's written report, but it was never given to her parents. (See Chapter 2)

Some months later, Marla began speaking spontaneously, and both parents were very much relieved.

They later returned with Marla to the clinic, when she was age 5, to see if the doctor thought she was ready for kindergarten. Although his team saw a continued lack of social aloofness, they did notice some mild improvement. Therefore, Dr. Hunt recommended that Marla have a kindergarten experience. What the clinicians thought was a social improvement may have been no more than a temporary, age-connected variance.

Born into a family with extreme, socially-conformist values, Marla's unsociable nature was unacceptable to them. Nevertheless, not knowing of her autism, Marla was brought-up by parents who expected her to blossom forth, as if she were an NT <u>neurotypical</u>* child.

Text:

During infancy and early childhood, I strongly resisted being physically held, touched, kissed or cuddled - an aloofness that must have discouraged my parents from displaying any normal affection. In addition, Mother did clerical work at home, so that I was left in a play-pen for hours on end, deprived of all muscle, nerve and sensory stimulation.

Though resisted by me, at the time, I needed what all children require: physical and verbal stimulation especially during infancy. For me to have tolerated hands-on stimulation, it had to be provided in an especially gentle, non-threatening way and in small doses.

During the first year of life, a considerable amount of brain development can be accomplished - even with autistics - if caregivers are sensitive to how much the baby will accept from them, in terms of physical contact and parental speech.

I've read that early childhood stimulation accelerates the brain to develop alternate nerve pathways and connections. These can then facilitate additional learning skills, so that I might have developed a wider range of thinking ability and a greater variety of interests.

Now as an adult, with <u>linear thinking</u>* and math my only strengths, I'm restricted as to how far I can progress in any scholarly subject, and now find myself lacking in interest, beyond the bare essentials of anything intellectual. (See Chapter 31 - Intellect and Chapter 5 - Attention-Deficit Disorder/Hyperactivity)

As previously noted, at age 3 and 3 months, lacking speech ability, I went with my parents to Dr. Brian Hunt's clinic for an evaluation. In his written report, he made mention of my aloofness and lack of sociality - noticed by himself and the other clinicians. Mainly because of my frigid social behavior, he diagnosed me as having autism but with intellectual potential. Although documented in his report, *there was no mention of autism, indicated to my parents, nor did they ever see the clinic report.* (See Chapter 2 - Autism)

Even though my coldness was not discussed with Dr. Hunt, my parents were troubled that I had not formed an emotional bond with either of them. Nevertheless, they looked upon my frigid behavior as an immaturity that would eventually normalize, just as my speech did.

They were never told I would always lack sociability in addition to other deficits in my personality; and of course they were never alerted to the formidable problems of raising a child with autism. As a result, with parents in denial that anything was permanently wrong with me, I was brought up with harsh discipline and ongoing rejection of my true essence - the human being I truly was!

As a mentally disturbed autistic child and fending for myself, I was enrolled in a public school kindergarten, at age 5.

By not suggesting a private school, Dr. Hunt must have believed that an integrated education was best for an autistic child, since I might develop social skills in being among normal children.

As I continued in public school, crowded classes deprived me of much needed individualized instruction. By having autism and personality disorders, instead of benefiting from my classmates, I was targeted with unfriendliness, teasing, and humiliation.

I carried myself differently and stood out from everyone in the room. Being immature, I would cry out when not getting what I wanted and also had a nervous habit of picking my nose.

Physically, I was overweight, had a face full of acne, and buck teeth (braces later improved them). My only quick-fix was to sit in the back of the room, trying to be less conspicuous.

Even though I avoided doing most class assignments, school standards were so pathetic, I still made passing grades.

I should never have been mainstreamed. I needed a private school education with small classes, a curriculum tailored to my learning ability and devoid of classmate harassment. While I had good math skills, I could not comprehend "people subjects" like history and literature. Had I been enrolled in a private school, with fewer students, the teacher might have given me individualized instruction, and utilized "non-people" reading material.

All during the school years, my autistic lack of human understanding prevented high marks in people subjects, although I did get A's in math and science. When evaluating a report card, my parents would get upset, not understanding the inconsistency of my grades. Early as age five, I was pre-occupied with my private language.

It consisted of made-up words for various inner feelings, special names for people in my life, and sundry words for important objects around me. In fact, it is a lexicon that has continued growing all my life. For example, if Father became ill, only by thinking of my private name for him would I experience the appropriate emotion. Without his special name, I would feel nothing.

In school, stuck with Dyspraxia, what I wanted more than anything, but lacked, were better functioning gross motor and fine motor skills. If playing a game required jumping, running or catching a ball, it was no fun being a klutz. (See Chapter 17)

My clumsiness was ridiculed by the other kids. Had there been early childhood intervention - with the right physiotherapist - I might have been taught some motor skill and ball playing ability. In addition, my hands could have become less clumsy when doing self-care, picking up small objects, doing kitchen chores, coloring a picture, handwriting, using food utensils, buttoning clothes, and countless other small muscle tasks. Because of receiving no treatment during the early formative years, when I had relative brain plasticity, my window of opportunity* will, forever, remain "shut."

I never felt any sadness having no friends, because neither the girls nor their activities were of interest to me. In contrast, Mother was adamant that I have playmates. She was aware that the girls I already knew made fun of me, so I wasn't obliged to play with them. However, if a new kid in my age bracket moved into the neighborhood, Mother invited her for a visit, desirous of a friendship developing. One never did and for each failure, I was blamed and soundly criticized.

Being a lone wolf, some of my solo childhood play consisted of dialing nonsense phone numbers and listening to various noise patterns. For example, any 3 digit exchange number followed by "55" produced a loud busy-signal that I dubbed "big busy," while an exchange number followed by "22" caused a low-volume signal that I named "little busy."

At about the age of 6, I was becoming increasingly adamant in regard to the family routines. Noticing that our suppers followed a weekly schedule, I felt a strong anticipation for each predictable meal. If the routine varied by day of the week or Mother's food choices, I would become unglued with a fit of temper.

Speaking of food, there were two routines that gave me delicious noshes of cakes and cookies: the Friday visit to my grandmother and the Sunday trip to Aunt Hilda. Should there be any change of plans, I would holler and stamp my feet.

I was once invited by a classmate to attend a movie. Since her timing would interfere with my Sunday lunch routine of poached eggs on toast, Mother became enraged when she heard me tell the girl: "I cannot go because it is time to eat my 'big lunch!'" Here I was turning down a potential friendship and Mother, infuriated, hollered "big lunch", in my face, over-and-over.

Being autistic, rotten luck gave me two parents obsessed with superficial values and social conformity. Whenever rebelling against having a circle of friends or wearing stylish clothes, I'd be severely reprimanded. In stark contrast, since my <u>NT</u>* sisters, <u>Sherry</u>* and <u>Linda</u>*, adapted to parental values, both lucked-out with a normal childhood.

My voracious eating habit infuriated both parents. They were sticklers for their three girls having slender figures When shopping for clothes, I remember Mother humiliating me in front of the saleslady, by announcing my need of a size larger dress than a girl my age would normally wear.

At home, I was criticized for daydreaming and not doing any exercise to work-off the extra pounds. As if Mother's scolding was not enough, I'd also get ridiculed by Sherry for having a huge appetite.

Both parents were angered by my hatred of social gatherings. They insisted I attend weddings, bowling parties, dances, concerts and even day camp. To resist going, my usual tantrums were mostly ignored; and as I had anticipated, the affairs were nothing but sheer boredom!

As an anti-social person, I was made to feel guilty and hated being the family "black sheep." Getting beaten-down emotionally and lacking self-confidence, I would sometimes feel deserving of their harsh criticism.

When Mother saw my freakishness, the time she had me do kitchen chores, it should have alerted her to my disabilities. (See Chapter 11 - Kitchen Chores and Self-Abuse) Instead, I was bawled-out for biting the kitchen counter and ripping a cloth towel to shreds with my teeth! On a similar note, whenever sitting at the family desk and doing hated school assignments, I would chew on the drawers and compartments. With all of the angry biting, my parents should have had me evaluated by a psychiatrist, but they never did.

I still recall an early age when Mother introduced me to ice skating. She did it lickety-split, planting me in the middle of an outdoor rink, leaving me alone while she quickly returned to the bench. With faulty body coordination and not having been taught to balance myself or glide on the ice, all I could do was crawl off the rink - embarrassed and frustrated. Wanting to ice skate - but given no instruction by her - the whole experience was stupid and thoughtless from the get-go. I've never figured out what Mother had in mind!

Although I loved to eat, I dreaded meals at the family table where I was often put through the third degree, as to what had transpired in school that day. Furthermore, whenever doing tics, I was humiliated by Mother's hollering and the family staring at me. She warned me that if the "disgusting tics" continued, I'd be locked up in my room. (See Chapter 6 - Tourette Syndrome)

To further instill fear, for doing uncontrollable tic behaviors, I was warned that unless the blinking stopped, I would surely go blind! And if the vocal noise tics did not cease, I could forever lose my voice! By Mother refusing to believe there was anything seriously wrong with me, she made no attempt to understand Tourette or, for that matter, any of my other disorders. She was strongly convinced my deviant behaviors were no more than bad habits, in need of correction and more discipline!

When arguments at home reached the boiling point and I needed someone to be supportive and take my side, there was not a soul I could call on; both my parents and Sherry were against me, while Linda never said much.

Nor did I get any assist from the extended family of grandparents, aunts, uncles or cousins. Concerned that I might disgrace the Comm image, my atypical personality was kept shrouded in secrecy. No relative was aware of my desperate need for psychological support*, tangible support* and simple human kindness.

In retrospect, had the relatives known of my predicament, I don't know how much good it would have done. They had values similar to my parents and were not the type of people to support non-conformist behavior, such as mine. Nevertheless, any moral support from even one of them could have made a difference; and without it, I had nobody.

My personality is a complex blending of two factors that go way beyond an autistic *disinterest* in people. Inborn neurological disorders and a disastrous childhood, both factors operating in <u>synergy</u>*, are responsible for my extreme *dislike* of humans. Even as an adult, being hyper-sensitive to someone's harsh words or mistreatment, I often wish the perpetrator dead!

If my parents had something called "nurturing intuition," they could have provided me with a warm-hearted family environment and whenever possible been supportive of my individuality. Instead, my true essence was rejected at every turn. Consequently, as a troubled youngster I became an even more troubled adolescent. With the right upbringing, I could have made a far better life-adjustment, with neutral feelings toward most people and not a general dislike of humanity!

Needless to say, their overbearing efforts of converting me into a social animal failed miserably. My being a done-deal, hardwired and inflexible, their psychological abuse only served to make me increasingly rebellious and non-conformist. I consider my upbringing a psychological disaster and in combination with the Montreal environment, these two factors are the ruination of my life. (See Chapter 9 - Montreal)

At age 14, I began weekly sessions with Dr. Hyman Freedman, psychiatrist. In a meeting with my parents, so as not to upset them, he avoided the autism diagnosis and referred to my neurological condition as <u>Asperger syndrome.</u>*

Preferring Dr. Freedman's less severe terminology, and despite my adolescent efforts to educate them, Mom and Dad remained steadfast in rejecting the autism label; as further evidence, they mistakenly believed my good intelligence disproved any possibility of having autism. (See Chapter 14 - Psychiatrist)

Throughout Mother's life, she steadfastly maintained that I was not autistic. As for Father, it is only quite recently, in his senior years, that he gives occasional lip service to my autism. (See Chapter 4)

In my late teens and early twenties, the few attempts I made at becoming a social person met with failure. In one such endeavor, at age 17, I went to a group psychotherapy meeting where several clients, led by a therapist, were encouraged to freely express their thoughts and emotions.

Prior to the meeting, I had a short conversation with a group member. A few minutes later, when the session began, she described to the group how artificial my comments had sounded: "It was as though Marla had flipped a switch and a *robot* began talking." Defenseless and not expecting her "stab in the back," in tears, I ran out of the session and never attended another one!

During the teens, my relationship with Mother seriously worsened. I had become more high-strung due to commonplace teen attitudes and hormonal, physical changes.

Frequently, I complained to Mother and Father about their late-night social gatherings that kept me awake for hours. Even when not having company, they played the radio or TV far too loud; my complaints were ignored and the noise continued.

The relationship at home continued to worsen, and Dr. Freedman aware of my unsolvable friction with the family, he suggested it was time I moved out and lived in my own place. With my family ties on the skids, both parents agreed it was the right decision.

Soon, thereafter, I moved to a dismal basement apartment; it was all I could afford!

Though having left the family nest, I could not escape Mother's wrath; she was soon contacted by the landlord, with complaints I'd busted up his kitchen!

In paying me a quick visit, she was horrified by the damage. Seething with anger and spewing forth invective for over an hour, she kept referring to me as a "mental case" - all the while nervously, chain-smoking a pack of cigarettes.

Living on my own, in a dump, was certainly no panacea.

CONCLUSION:
Marla was born with multiple neurological disorders, including severe autism. She had an upbringing with parents who denied the seriousness and permanence of her condition. They thought with Marla's fine intelligence, she would gradually learn to behave as a normal person. Actually, her disorders were neurologically <u>hardwired</u>*; over time, they tended toward increased severity rather than improvement.

Marla's dysfunctional childhood and worsening teen years demonstrate the power of human illusion, i.e. parents in a world of fantasy, in *total denial*, of their daughter's unrelenting, true condition.

What follows is a chapter related to Marla's autism and how it has affected her life.

2

Autism

INTRODUCTION:
Marla's lack of social feeling, her rigid routines, problematic language, poor imagination, extreme inflexibility, repetitive tendencies, and ritualistic behaviors - these are traits often consistent with a diagnosis of autism.

Autism is often referred to as a "spectrum disorder," meaning that each of its individual traits can, individually, range from mild to severe. The usual and most profound indicator, common to an autism diagnosis, is the inability and/or lack of interest in relating to people.

Autism can be the result of a genetic disorder or trauma to the fetus, caused by drugs, hormone injections and other substances ingested by the mother; these occur during or prior to gestation. Illness and other adverse events during pregnancy can injure the fetus. Insufficient oxygen or forceps damage during the birthing procedure are also potential hazards.

Any of the aforementioned factors can damage areas of the brain and result in autism - a lifelong disorder without a cure.

Note:

As previously mentioned, Dr. Brian Hunt, a psychiatrist, diagnosed Marla as having HFA high functioning autism*. The reader should keep in mind that HFA is not related to the severity of one's autism; it is a label pertaining solely to the *co-existing* level of the person's intelligence, ranging from normal to high and even gifted. For example, Marla suffers from severe autism that co-exists with high intelligence.

Text:

My autistic brain disorder, affecting early childhood development, set me apart with impairments in social behavior, extreme inflexibility, problems with verbal interaction, lack of imagination and much more. Mentally, I lived in a world of my own - aloof and disinterested in the people around me.

Prior to and during her pregnancy, Mother was taking fertility hormone injections. It is reasonable to hypothesize that her medication caused damage to brain structures during my fetal development - translating into autism and other dysfunctions.

According to family history, my autism has no apparent genetic basis; and I might add, my two siblings were not autistic.

During my infancy, there were early traits of autism. I behaved as though deaf - ignoring anyone talking or making sounds; instead, I would bang my head on sides of the crib and playpen.

Neither parent was terribly concerned about my lack of interest in them, believing it was an immaturity I'd surely outgrow. Throughout childhood, I continued with unnatural, aloof behavior. Yet, because of my good intelligence and their training, they believed I would outgrow the aloofness and learn social decorum. There was no warning or understanding that my disinterest in relating to people would, in fact, be a lifelong consequence of having an autistic disorder.

I fault Dr. Hunt for not making his diagnosis of autism known to my parents. He should have also prepared them for the likelihood that later in life, as an autistic adult, I would need their moral and tangible support.

During my upbringing, there were battles with my mother over the stylish but impractical clothes she expected me to wear. My lack of sociality included a disinterest in my appearance, since I had no need to impress anyone with my outfits nor did I care, in the least, what anybody else wore. With no interest in clothing styles and colors, all that mattered was comfort, ample pockets and convenience when getting dressed and undressed.

Being sticklers for maintaining an impeccable family image, both parents made sure that my quirky behaviors were well-hidden from the relatives and friends of the family. Since I was not conforming to the social code, my parents were fearful of "letting my personality out of the closet," afraid others would learn of my mental problems and think less of us. Yet, had I been socially normal but with a club foot, my parents would have freely talked about my handicap since, in their estimation, a physical disability was not shameful.

Nowadays, as an adult with autism, in desperate need of support from the extended family or my parents' close friends - these people hardly know I exist.

Because of autism, I never had a real friend; no acquaintance ever lasted more than one or two get-togethers. While this upset my parents, I was a true loner and preferred solitude.

Atypical facial expressions, body movements and physical gestures are easily misunderstood, so that my unusual autistic body language might cause others to react with annoyance, teasing and sometimes harassment.

Symptoms of my autism are intensified by their synergy with overlapping neurological disorders, such as: Attention-Deficit Disorder and Executive Function Disorder. (See Chapters 5 and 20, respectively)

By having a disinterest in people, I cannot derive pleasure from reading novels or watching movies and sitcoms on TV. As for a medical drama, I'm only interested in the sickness and treatment aspects, never the love angle or any other human relationship, emotions I can never understand.

Adult autism can be easily misunderstood. For someone who doesn't really know me, the aloofness and moody demeanor often gets perceived as a personal insult. Consequently, others may verbally fault me for not being warm and friendly. In response, I readily put the onus on myself, by saying: "It is fine for you to be sociable, but I have a condition that renders me unable to establish relationships with people."

Acquaintances like to advocate their religion as a solution to my problems. So as not to hurt their feelings, I have a stock answer: "My non-belief in a Higher Power is caused by a learning disability, preventing me from having the kind of Faith that is required."

My inflexibility prevents me from developing new interests. I'm living in an era when the very things I do enjoy often become unavailable; whereas the ones I thoroughly despise become more popular. For example, outdoor biking, in Montreal, is increasingly prevented by inclement weather, due to climate change. Yet whiny music that I find intolerable - blasting on radio, TV and in retail stores - has become all the rage, a pop-culture obsession! (See Chapter 9)

Compartmentalization is the ability to *split off* from everything not germane and focus one's full attention on something specific. Because of other thoughts "stuck" in my mind, I mostly find it impossible to "split off" and compartmentalize my thinking.

My tolerating an individual is possible only when there is a special common interest, or if the person is offering psychological or tangible support. Otherwise, any kind of close relationship cannot exist.

I had an autistic speech delay in early childhood, until the beginning of age 4 (See Chapter 1 - Childhood) Also, symptomatic of autism, I still have <u>voice inflection</u>* problems and deficits in the social use of language. I find it difficult to have an informal discussion with anyone. I tend to ramble on about my own problems and with little, or no, interest in what the other person has to say.

I also believe that autism is mostly responsible for my inability to recognize and understand humor. (See Chapter 24 - Humor)

By lacking imagination - a trait of autism - I have trouble dealing with life's daily problems and lack the ability to be resourceful.

With overly literal autistic thinking, when feeling threatened by something terrible that may happen or a crisis already in progress, I lose my composure and suffer from panic. At times, there is even an emotional breakdown of crying, screaming, biting my arms, stomping my feet and other traits of childhood regression. (See Chapter 7 - Anxiety and Meltdowns)

Chronic worry and anxiety are traits symptomatic of both autism and Tourette Syndrome. By working in synergy, they can give me a sense of extreme foreboding. (See Chapter 6)

When reading text, I cannot distinguish between the main idea and the less important details; they all seem about equal. I typically latch onto every tiny detail, but miss the overall plot; it is caused by lack of central coherence, a trait of autism.

Variations recommended by anyone are rejected. My autism and personality disorders create a synergy of compulsive adherence to routines; people's suggestions are automatically shot down.

During high school, I loved and excelled in chemistry because it dealt with the periodic table of atomic elements that fed my fascination with fixed patterns and regularity; in that regard, my linear ability paid off!

Another autistic trait of value has always been my desire to locate certain linear patterns and consistencies in subject matter. It is one reason I was drawn to mathematics throughout the school years and later as my college major. Seeking fixed, linear sequences is also an asset at work, where I devise shortcuts on the computer to automate some of the data-entry material that requires processing.

Many of the mildly afflicted autistic individuals, with whom I've corresponded, consider autism as simply a different way of thinking - something akin to living in a different culture. As with many spectrum people,* they believe autism is a *gift* that society should learn to appreciate. Leaving aside my math and computer skills, unlike these mildly autistic people, I openly admit to having a severe academic handicap - caused by autism. Most glaring are my inabilities to deal with literature, history, foreign languages and any other people subjects.

As we know, some individuals are "fighters" who are driven to push themselves while others lack the motivation. Autistic people with moderate disorders, who have fighter instincts, reject their dysfunctional behavior and will push themselves to work on social skills and other weaknesses. With my full-blown autism, I cannot be a fighter or involve myself beyond life's essential routines that overburden me, more than ever, in this millennium!

Perhaps I do myself a disservice, by making comparisons with other autistic people. My horrible life adjustment is the result of much more than autism. An abrasive childhood did not help matters. I also suffer from other neurological disorders and personality traits which add depth and complexity to the nature of my autism. (See Chapter 21 - Co-morbid)

As a teenager, I began seeing my Psychiatrist, Dr. Hyman Freedman, on a weekly basis. With his supportive therapy and much kindness, the relationship continued for three decades, until it all stopped due to his fatal illness, when I was age 47. (See Chapter 14)

I've suffered from two examples of professional negligence: Dr. Hunt failed me when I was a toddler, by not telling my parents of my autism - allowing them to believe that a developmental lag, in speaking ability, was my only dysfunction.

In my teens, Dr. Freedman also failed me, remiss in not making understandable to my parents the seriousness of my autism. Instead, he would only refer to my condition as <u>Asperger syndrome</u>*, a mild offshoot of autism. Consequently, they mistakenly believed that my quirky behaviors would one day normalize and I'd become the daughter they always wanted.

Led astray by two psychiatrists, both parents remained forever in denial, not believing that my dysfunctional personality was a <u>hardwired</u>* reality that could never change. Now, as an adult, with only my father's sporadic support, life has become extremely problematic, in fending for myself.

Unable to "play the role" of a normal person, I've had to sustain, all my life, endless barrages of parental criticism. I was never able to alter their naiveté, a false belief that if I chose to, I could become, ipso facto, an <u>NT</u>* person.

I recall a therapy session, in my 30's, when Dr. Freedman off-handedly remarked that when I was a teenager, he suspected that I might have future difficulties keeping a job and fulfilling my adult responsibilities. He further said that I might require my parents' psychological and tangible support, throughout my adult life! Was a word of this ever mentioned to them? No! Have I needed their full support? Yes! Am I suffering with its gross inadequacy? Yes! In just thinking about it, am I damn mad? You bet!

Usually, my father finds it inconvenient to telephone me in the evening. I must have a conversation with him - essentially - to discuss thoughts and emotions of my day's happenings. Without it, the night's sleep is restless and choppy. Most evenings, I am left high-and-dry, *without* his phone call!

For psychological support* or material support* in this millennium, I get crumbs from Father and zilch from others; I have yet to meet a Good Samaritan.

Except for an intermittent car ride with my father, I get no tangible help. In a city of two million, there's not a soul I can depend on! My fondest wish is vacating Montreal and moving to a small city - where examples of kindness and human decency still prevail.

CONCLUSION:
Clearly, Marla has suffered from severe autism. It is further complicated by co-morbid disorders that were never treated and with parents in denial that anything was genuinely wrong with her.

Verbal abuse and punishment were her parents sole *teaching methods* and destined to fail because of Marla's personality - hardwired, resolute and not susceptible to change. As an adult, she is a lone voice crying in the wilderness, with virtually no support.

Note:

By studying several major brain structures, implicated with autism, researchers have discovered that autistic brains may lack adequate connections among the following:

**Cerebral cortex which is the outer layer of the brain. It is where thought processes take place; responsible for speech, movement, perception, memory and other functions;

**Amygdala controls emotions and aggressive behavior;

**Hippocampus is important for learning and memory;

**Basal ganglia is involved in motor control and movement;

**Cerebrum functions include speech, memory, vision, personality and some muscle control;

**Cerebellum is responsible for fine-tuning motor activity and regulating balance, body movements, coordination and the muscles used in speaking;

**Brain stem serves as a relay station, passing messages to various parts of the body;

**Corpus callosum is a thick band of nerve fibers connecting the two hemispheres;

In the autistic brain, some of the structures do not function in proper unison; the needed connections are either weak or missing.

What follows is the story of a mother who rejected and verbally abused her autistic daughter, for the youngster's "own good."

3

Mother

INTRODUCTION:
Mrs. Millie Comm gave birth to Marla, her first child, on July 15, 1956. She was then faced with the difficult task of raising an aloof infant who resisted being touched or cuddled. The woman's highly sociable temperament was totally at odds with Marla's extremely introverted personality. Mrs. Comm, however, remained steadfast in the belief that it was nothing more than a temporary, childish aberration. (See Autism - Chapter 2)

Text:
Mother was convinced that my unsociable behavior was deliberate and that strict discipline was required to change my traits. By not seeking professional counsel, she never learned that I should have been treated with finesse instead of angry disapproval. I believe her harsh methods permanently damaged my self-esteem and made my negative feelings for people - even more hateful.

She refused to budge one iota, from what she believed was "proper" social decorum. Nor would she relinquish the verbal abuse and hollering, to have me become the daughter she always wanted.

Now as an adult, in retrospect, had I been treated with kindness, I might have developed positive feelings for Mother, my first human relationship; instead, her maltreatment and verbal abuse were counter-productive.

Beneath gestures of occasional tolerance, I could detect her smoldering anger and resentment; she looked upon me as nothing but trouble. I was the daughter she never enjoyed, while Sherry and Linda gave her much pleasure. On the other hand, Mother had a strong sense of duty, never giving up on my learning to become a sociable person.

In raising my two younger siblings, born a few years after me, she was an exemplary parent to both NT neurotypical* girls, since their behaviors were in lockstep with both parents.

Because my neurological disorders were invisible to the eye, Mother gave them no credence; also, my apparent smartness seemed to contradict any problems in mental development. (See Chapter 21 - Invisible)

I was disciplined for a variety of behaviors. For instance, she would threaten to lock me in my room, if I didn't stop doing tics, (See Chapter 6 -Tourette Syndrome).

Mother had what I call a *time bomb* persona; she always seemed peeved, with me, about something. Sensing her irritability and asking what I had done wrong, she'd answer, "Nothing." As a result, I would feel uneasy, never knowing when the build-up of her anger would explode!

The problems with kitchen chores began at age 7, when I was first required to help with the cleanup. When Mother saw me biting the work table or dropping a dish, I'd get verbally blasted with her anger. (See Chapter 11 - Kitchen Chores) Despite my poor functioning, Mother kept insisting I do my share of the work. Because she never considered me physically incapacitated; I was held responsible for everything I broke. Despite being chastised for the weird biting and being such a klutz, try as I did, I could not do any better. The breakage, spills and biting continued despite her tongue lashings. (See Chapter 17 - Dyspraxia)

Never experimenting with a kinder and gentler approach, Mother believed that *mollycoddling* did nothing but reinforce unwanted behaviors. Father in lockstep concurred with her thinking.

Her personality was all love and caring for my late sister Linda who was diagnosed with cancer at age 15. By age 18, she was wheelchair bound with terminal cancer, a condition with *visible* evidence. In contrast, my autism and co-morbid disorders were *invisible* - well-hidden inside the brain - so that Mother refused to believe they even existed! (See Chapter 21 - Invisible)

I had to endure another mistreatment. As a way of secretly keeping tabs on me, Mother used a *spy network*. Relatives and friends, who lived in our general vicinity, were told to report anything unusual related to me. They would tattle to mother about my hitchhiking a ride, scavenging for food, and anything else that seemed improper. If one of her spies saw me having an emotional meltdown, it was also made known to my parents. (See Chapter 7 - Meltdowns)

For a time, Mother and I used the same hairdresser who once mistook my dandruff for minuscule insects! Instead of telling me about it, she played the role of informer, by tattling to my mother: "Mrs. Comm, I saw a disgusting infestation of *lice* in Marla's hair!"

When I was age 22, Mother was eager to pay for my psychoanalysis, having been told it would solve unconscious impulses, anxieties, and internal conflicts - all resulting from early childhood trauma.

As if by magic, she presumed I would surely discard my atypical personality and emerge a socially acceptable person. In addition, by *freeing* my energy for mature affection, she envisioned me with new-found friends, dating, marriage and babies - the whole nine yards!

There were problems with her scenario: My brain dysfunctions were inborn, hardwired and not caused by early childhood trauma. The two years of psychoanalysis resolved nothing; they were a misuse of time and money!

Whenever Mother did me a substantial favor, there was always an undercurrent of anger. To her credit, she was intent on getting me out of a noisy, poorly maintained condo apartment where I then lived, along with the kitchen I had wrecked. In her threatening tone of voice, I was given notice: "Having screwed-up every other place you've lived in, things had better work out, normally, in the up-scale condo I have in mind."

True to her word, Mother helped finance, in 1998, an elegant condo apartment, along with fine furniture and stylish clothes. What had often been her angry tone of voice, now became a scare tactic along with the threat of abandonment! Specifically, if any damage was done to my fine condo, she and Father would forever vacate Montreal, and no longer have anything to do with me!

The clothes consisted of styles I refused to wear and were returned. Hundreds of dollars were spent on new furniture which I did not need. Presumably, all the finery in her thinking contained the romantic twist of an eventual suitor, being impressed by my attractive lifestyle. She failed to realize that nothing was more noxious, to me, than needless luxury and the thought of becoming her sociable makeover.

My parents were willing to waste money on trappings for which I had no use. Yet, at the same time, continued their policy of not making arrangements for car rides and psychological support when they traveled out of town. Only intent on superficial values, neither parent cared about my *true* needs.

Though we had extreme differences on most issues, Mother and I thoroughly hated Montreal winters. More than once, she expressed the dream of taking a trip with my father, as <u>snowbirds</u>* and escape to Florida, throughout the bitterly cold winter months. If while they were gone, back-up support had been arranged for me, I would never oppose their trip; yet this vital need, for getting support, was always "shot down" by them.

My appearance was critically important to Mother. Whenever I visited the family home, all that mattered were my clothes - not the daughter wearing them. When greeting her, she ignored what I said but always made comments about the way I was dressed and with rare exception, always found fault.

When I was age 25, I recall buying a down-filled jacket at a bargain price. My parents hated its orange color and kept bugging me to throw it out! Because of their unrelenting pressure, I had to get rid of it. Mother ended up buying me a far more expensive jacket, but I would have much preferred the other one. Although it did not meet my parents standard for appearance, it was the warmest and most practical one I ever owned; for instance, it had straight pockets which I preferred to the "stylish," slanted ones, with things always falling out of them!

Mother was also a stickler for traditional functions. Upon my sister Linda's untimely death at age 19, Mother was angry with me for not <u>sitting Shiva</u>* the full number of hours every day! She kept her fury bottled up, but a few years later allowed it to explode.

I set off the "bombshell" by refusing to attend my sister Sherry's wedding. Mother threatened to cut me off from the family if I refrained from going; in addition, she would have me fired from the nursing home where we both worked. This emotional blackmail got her what she wanted because the thought of being left with no parents and losing my job, had me intimidated - allowing me no other choice but to attend the wedding!

My California pen-pal characterized my mother as a highly complex woman - in many ways a wonderful wife and mother - but with a *dark side*. It was a wise insight because when Mother's discipline failed to improve my attitude, a dark side spewed forth with anger and words belittling me. In contrast, by having an extremely sociable personality and able to conceal her dark side, friends and relatives thought the world of her.

In tenth grade my purse was stolen and I refused - against Mother's wishes - to retrieve a junky watch that had been found. Since possessions far more important were taken, the timepiece seemed worthless by comparison. Nevertheless, my mother became enraged over the watch and we quarreled bitterly. In the midst of her non-stop verbal abuse, a friend called on the phone and, as if by magic, Mother's words became sugary sweet. A few minutes later, she put down the phone and without missing a beat, her dark side returned, viciously scolding me, as before.

One day, during another fight, Mother was enraged to the point I could no longer take her screaming. Terribly overwrought, I ran down the basement steps and using the extension phone, I called my psychiatrist. Listening from upstairs, she overheard me ask his secretary if I could speak with him. Mother then raced down the steps and yanked the phone from my hand. She hated the idea of my complaining to anyone outside the family and considered it a breach of Comm privacy.

Mother's fixation, with what she believed was *normal behavior,* did not allow for deviation. She was determined to force-feed her conventional values down my throat. However, in opposing her with my own set of behaviors, I marched to a different drummer (See Chapter 27 - Oppositional Defiant Disorder). Speaking of a different drummer, I recall threats of being grounded after school if I dared continue with the <u>Jesus cult</u>*. (See Chapter 8 - Meditation)

Since I refused to comply with her expectations, my upbringing was a disaster. By pressuring me to adopt a conventional lifestyle of fiddly clothes, best friends, social affairs, dating guys, etc. - in conflict with my personality - Mother's nudging, needling and threatening almost destroyed me.

I always felt like worthless scum, especially the time Mother announced that I should be committed to Montreal's notorious Douglas Schizophrenia Hospital - for the mentally ill. While always suspecting she never loved me, those poisonous words clinched it! Both Dr. Freedman and my current psychiatrist counseled me not to take her threats seriously; they were nothing more than empty hot air. That may be the case, but it was still cruel treatment because with autism, I have a tendency to take spoken words *literally* and fail to "read" people's true intentions - a skill that has always escaped me. (See Chapter 24 - Theory of Mind)

Since I'm an oddball with countless defects, I've wondered if she ever regretted not aborting me. When broaching the subject, she was incensed that I could even suggest such a possibility!

Because of her closeness with Sherry and Linda, born a few years after me, she should not be judged an outright bad mother. While affection for me was non-existent, my NT sisters fell in lockstep with her societal values, thereby earning her love and approval; because of the disparity, I have to admit that feelings of jealousy sometimes gnawed at me!

I discussed with Dr. Freedman the dysfunctional relationship I had with Mother. He agreed there were shortcomings, such as her obsession with clothing choices and maligning me for doing tics. I recall him once saying that my parents *loved* me but did not *like* me. Since their demeanor did not reflect *love*, I disagreed with him.

Mother blamed me for the worsening of my menstrual cycle; known to be affected by one's state of mind. Case in point was her hollering at me, in my teens, when I was ill with an exceptionally heavy flow. While criticized for not *controlling* my emotions, she never taught me how to do it.

Another example were the migraine headaches which Mother said I deliberately caused by not learning how to cope with stress. Once again it was all talk and zilch instruction!

When I discussed Mother's mistreatment of me with my current shrink, he characterized her as having been mentally ill. I disagreed, because she was well-liked, had no bizarre behaviors and no bad relationships, other than a dysfunctional connection with me.

Lacking techniques in how to raise an autistic child, Mother had always been in need of counseling. However, being a private individual, she would avoid discussing personal problems with an outsider - not even a mental health professional! Moreover, being in denial, neither did she believe there was anything incurable about my quirky behavior nor would it serve any purpose to learn about autism. There was never a questioning attitude in trying to understand my strange personality, never an awareness that it was based on mental processes, hardwired and unrelenting.

CONCLUSION:
Marla's parents received no counseling on how to raise a child with autism and other handicaps. Nor was it believed by her mother, in total denial, that anything was neurologically amiss with her daughter.

Marla's *asocial* personality was kept well-hidden from the family's social network. Mom and Dad were fearful it could somehow damage their well-thought-of Comm reputation.

Next is a depiction of her father whose treatment of Marla was in lockstep with that of her mother.

4

Father

INTRODUCTION:
Mrs. Comm was dominant in Marla's upbringing and Mr. Comm was in full agreement with the discipline being used. In a tragic house fire, January 28, 2000, he suffered the loss of his wife (see Chapter 36- Mother's Death). Now, with his wife gone, he became Marla's only potential support person.

Text:
Father has been terribly lonely without my mother. To compensate, he seeks frequent male and female get-togethers. I believe his active social life has an obsessive quality, designed to lessen the pain of her death.

He is with cronies most every night; a whirlwind social life without any concern for my needs. The nightly phone call - I must have for his support - cannot be relied on. The next day he will use an excuse that no telephone was available or that he simply forgot. He also insists that it's rude making a phone call, with time away from his friends, when they are out socializing.

I remember a night of sheer terror because the television news was full of reports about an anthrax attack following the 9/11 catastrophe! I desperately needed to speak with Father and since he knew how vulnerable I am to reports of a crisis, I thought he would surely telephone me, but he never did.

I prefer speaking to him late in the evening, knowing that any stressors of the day are behind me. I can then share with him, what's on my mind, before retiring for the night and am able to sleep more peacefully.

As my only pillar of support and Father knowing this, the evening phone call should be a must. Because his calls are not reliable, my suffering is far worse than it need be. As a disabled daughter living alone, I ought to be uppermost in his mind with regular phone calls.

It's not that I resent his socializing because if he found the time to call me, I wouldn't care how he spent the evening. He often stays out until the wee hours and sleeps-in late the next day, so that my planning for a morning conversation is no more reliable than one the previous evening.

His social life gives me cause for worry; either a new wife or lady friend may come on the scene - someone who would monopolize his life and treat me harshly.

He has developed an interest in the crime programs on TV, so that when I phone him, he will not talk to me because "Law and Order" or a similar show is on. Consequently, we rarely have a conversation even on those nights he remains at home.

In candor, I know the real bone of contention for his not calling me; he cannot stomach the negativity of my personality. With all my difficulties - some neurological and others environmental - rarely are there any good-hearted or favorable topics to discuss with him.

If we're on the phone and I'm mentioning more problems than suit his patience, he will sarcastically interject: "What else is new?" Those words easily terminate the conversation. Being in great need of an understanding, tolerant support person, it is an obligation Father resists. With my tough luck, I have nobody else!

Unlike my mother, and since her passing, Father is not ashamed to tell people I'm autistic. Yet, despite having read magazine articles on the topic of Autism and much explaining by me, he has no solid understanding of my condition. Though he may give lip service to the word "autism," the true essence of my disability is mostly lost on him. As for my other disabilities, he exhibits even less understanding. (See Chapter 2)

To others, Father explains my HFA* as a daughter who is socially inept but a *genius* in other ways. To enhance his own ego, he paints the same false picture with relatives as he does with friends. While he proudly tells people that I'm self-supporting and live independently, he keeps my desperate need for tangible and psychological support strictly out of the conversation, nor does he talk about my impaired neurological functioning - getting progressively worse!

While Father considers me an underachiever, at the same time he brags to others about my math ability, college degree, medical librarian job and creative poetry. It must lead people to surmise: "You have to admire Marla; just think of how much she's accomplished, even with autism." Having people consider me a success story, gives the false impression that I am fully independent. Nothing could be further from the truth. Occasional car rides, the evening phone call and psychological support are all necessities - of which I get nothing from my father but a few crumbs! In fact, they only occur when he has nothing better to do; my needs rarely, if ever, take precedence.

Since I'm a college graduate, Father rationalizes I am, ipso facto, capable of functioning as a fully independent person; so that even a professional career is possible. I'm expected to solve my own problems with minimal support from him - his impossible dream!

What he also fails to consider is all the neurological baggage I contend with - so that a professional career was never an option. Part-time library work, in a geriatric nursing home, is the best I can muster; even that is exhausting and fraught with people problems.

With my job so enervating and stressful, I often talk about quitting and trying to get on disability. Living with the stigma of his daughter on public assistance, is an idea repugnant to him. To maintain his *all-important* Comm image, he considers my employment the foundation of an independent life, and keeps our family reputation well-thought-of.

As abrasive and harsh as she was, Mother understood at some level that my holding down a job did not come easy. During a spate of bad weather, if a nice day occurred she sometimes suggested I go biking and would reimburse my loss of salary. Years ago, besides working as a nurse's aide, I took courses at the university. At times, when I felt overwhelmed, Mother would have me take the day off and she'd compensate any loss of income. To give me a morning off, for what has become *job burnout*, Father has never made a similar gesture. (See Chapter 23 - Chronic Nervous Fatigue)

About the only kind of tangible support forthcoming from my parent is an occasional car ride to <u>Mt. Royal</u>*, but only at his convenience, when there is nothing else he prefers doing.

Father takes weeklong trips out of town, during the winter months, when I need his help the most. Yet, he spurns the idea of building a <u>support network</u>* nor does he make any effort to arrange for a backup person while he's away. I am left high-and-dry without necessities such as car rides or someone to "talk me" through a terrifying electrical storm or power outage, should one occur. (See Chapter 7 - Anxiety and Meltdowns)

Father becomes furious whenever I suggest a support network, volunteered by friends and relatives; in fact, it should have been sought decades ago, but never was. Father knows that my only option on winter days, when he's away, is to vegetate in bed. A mind is a terrible thing to waste and when reminded of this, all he does is get annoyed! (See Chapter 12 - Exercise)

Since fresh produce and dairy products are outrageously expensive, I've complained to him about high food prices, beyond my ability to afford them. What followed was the type of advice meant for a normal daughter: "You must accept changing conditions and learn to enjoy other foods when the ones you need are either unavailable or too costly." I told him that asking me to accept changes vital to my lifestyle is like asking an amputee to walk without legs. I reminded him that my autism would cause any substitution to be painful, often impossible, and suggested that he also take into account my essential dietary needs (See Chapter 10 - Food Shopping).

When he pooh-poohed my explanation, I recommended that he contact my social worker who would help him better understand my autism inflexibility - a suggestion he immediately shot down.

My father, in his senior years, will occasionally offer a ridiculous suggestion, such as telling me to buy a car and learn how to drive. He apparently blocks from his mind my poor hand-eye coordination. (See Chapter 17 - Dyspraxia) He also forgets that with a part-time job, on a small income, I lack the resources to afford healthful food - let alone buy and maintain a vehicle!

In this new millennium, he will agree that the world has gone haywire; yet, at the same time, he says I must learn to cope with life's difficult situations, whatever is dished out. He then wonders how a bright person, like me, can worry about remote possibilities such as food shortages, gas rationing, acts of terrorism and biological warfare - gloom and doom that he says may *never* happen.

Due to a heightened sensitivity, I react to crisis-news articles with greater fear than most people. By now, Father should know that my insecurities have nothing to do with intelligence; they are emotional reactions to threats of terrorism and world cataclysm. By telling me I should learn to cope and not fear a world that could prevent my normal lifestyle - he does not realize that without my daily routines, defining who I am, my life would be over! (See Chapter 35 - Suicidal Thoughts and Chapter 34 - The Quickening)

When telling Father about one of my heated squabbles occurring in a grocery store, he reproaches me for picking a fight. Even if a rude incident provoked my anger, he says I need to control my emotions. This is easier said than done, for a person with my neurological disorders. If I'm treated badly, there is an uncontrollable need to retaliate with my venomous language, spewing forth.

In a good mood, Father will admit that the workplace and city of Montreal conflict with my basic needs; and wishes he had the money to get me established, in a locale, that better suits my life style.

At other times, the debilitating nature of my job is lost on him. He mistakenly believes that working four mornings a week, in a nursing home library, is a "piece of cake." He fails to recognize the lack of support I'm given in the workplace, and this millennium's increased volume of work that makes the job impossibly demanding. (See Chapter 26 - Medical Library Assistant) The teasing and harassment I get from co-workers also fuels my dissatisfaction.

Ordinary tasks, that others take for granted, cause a disabled person, like me, to work much harder. Other than librarian responsibilities, what further depletes my energy level is the daily struggle of doing self-care and domestic chores. See Chapter 11 - Kitchen Chores and Chapter 20 - Executive Function Disorder)

I had learned that the Canadian government would no longer allow mentally ill people and those with neuro-psychiatric disorders to qualify for a personal income tax credit. As a result, I planned to write a protest e-mail to the Montreal Gazette that I hoped would go in their Letter to the Editor column. In mentioning this to Father, he angrily responded: "You don't have to announce to the whole world you are disabled and qualify for a disability tax credit."

When Mother was alive, they both concealed from everyone the "stigma" of a mentally disabled daughter; an embarrassment that still lurks in his mind, but to a somewhat lesser degree.

If he talks about a planned trip, the fear of having no support while he's away, gives me pangs of anxiety. His getaway can be for a weeklong religious holiday or a family event. Watching him glow with anticipation, yet feeling my own repugnance, makes me feel like a freak of nature!

What bugs me is that Father knows I have no interest in hearing news about my sibling in Toronto, yet anecdotes about her family never cease. He's hoping, one day, I'll patch up the relationship, but I never will.

Should he visit my apartment, I am always on edge, not wanting to hear comments about what I'm wearing or clutter all over the place. I also prefer that he not see my chewed-up arms that inevitably cause a quarrel. (See Chapter 11 - Self-Abuse)

As a kid, I was occasionally asked to help my father with handyman chores. Poorly coordinated, I had trouble doing what he wanted and with an Attention Deficit Disorder, I often misunderstood his instructions. Noticing I did something wrong, he would angrily bark his disapproval, making me even more clumsy. (See Chapter 5)

While other family members may have tolerated his quick temper, I was an oversensitive daughter with neuro-disorders*, and needed a father capable of patience and kindness.

With Mother's demise, Dr. Freedman and a grief counselor both advised my father to live his own life and travel at will. They adhered to the belief that parents are no longer obliged to help children who reach adulthood. I totally disagree because to survive as a functioning adult, fending for myself, I require limited but essential ongoing support.

I believe that my father does need his freedom to go on trips. However, I cannot help but be angry at his refusal to arrange for backup support, during periods when he's away, i.e. someone with understanding to speak with me on the phone, and provide an occasional car ride, as needed

CONCLUSION:

Mr. Comm has always been in varying amounts of denial that anything was neurologically wrong with Marla. Their relationship has been one of frequent misunderstanding and he's often hypercritical of his daughter.

Because of severe autism, Marla lacked the ability to form an emotional bond with either parent.

In recent years, despite a somewhat improved relationship, father and daughter still have different values, poles apart.

Marla fears her father's eventual passing, leaving her without his intermittent support; there is *nobody* to take his place!

The following chapter explains Marla's attention deficit disorder: the inattention, lack of focus, hyperactivity and impulsivity.

5

Attention Deficit Disorder/ Hyperactivity

INTRODUCTION:
Marla's attention deficit disorder/hyperactivity (ADD/H) is a neurological handicap characterized by the following traits: short attention span, distractibility, restlessness, impulsivity, poor organizational skill and quick to anger. It was a disorder apparent in early childhood and has continued all her life.

Text:
I have always been a fidgety, restless and nervous type which is partly explained by the hyperactivity in my ADD/H disorder. When I'm in a usual sitting position, dentists and hairdressers find me difficult to work with. I frequently squirm, shift positions and adjust my legs. At work, I can only remain seated and on task for short periods of time.

Especially at home, often times I am unable to finish whatever I'm doing through to completion. Not able to remain focused, my mind begins to wander uncontrollably.

I've never been able to focus on a task for more than ten or fifteen minutes, unless having a snack or eating a meal. This is a limitation that occurs whether reading an article, watching a TV documentary, studying for a course, creating a poem or composing an e-mail.

When finishing a regular meal, I won't feel like eating any more of it; but unless chomping-away on the enjoyment of a light snack, it is impossible to concentrate on anything intellectually demanding. For me, snacking satisfies the sensory pleasures of taste, texture, chewing and swallowing - all of which I enjoy.

While snacking does facilitate concentration, it is not the kind of trait one can do for hours on end because of health reasons. Our body was not made for continuous noshing but, for short periods, nothing else maintains focus and keeps me on task.

In class, boys with ADD/H tend toward overt, acting-out misbehavior. Hyperactive girls, with less aggressive hormones, may go unnoticed and undiagnosed throughout the school year, which was true in my case. During twelve years of public schooling, I did not seriously misbehave. The teachers ignored my hyperactive ADD, except for a single report card notation: "Needs improvement in attentiveness."

I was never hyperactive in disruptive ways, such as getting out of my seat or disturbing others but would sometimes, uncontrollably blurt out the answer to a question before the teacher could finish asking it!

In elementary school, the curriculum was shallow and repetitive so that a short attention span did not cause my grades to drastically suffer. To concentrate on homework, it was necessary to nibble on something even when doing math, my favorite subject.

As an adult, my reading habit is based mainly on medical and scientific topics of interest in reference material. Due to limited attention span, I am unable to devour entire books and lengthy articles in a few sittings. Whatever reading I do, must occur on-and-off in short sessions. When attempting to read a lengthy, technical article, I begin to daydream

Because of ADD/H, I lack the patience to read tedious instruction manuals that accompany appliances and electronic devices. Instead, I use trial and error plus common sense.

Despite lifelong ADD/H, I've accumulated a wide-ranging knowledge of neurological disorders, medical information and meteorology phenomena. Most of it is retained by an exceptionally good long-term memory and strong interest in the topics. Whatever I do know is not the result of in-depth comprehensive study, but rather an accumulation of fragmented knowledge, gleaned over time.

As a person easily bored, I cannot tolerate a physical exercise that is dull and tedious, such as walking a treadmill, pedaling an indoor bike, climbing flights of stairs or walking on flat ground. In contrast, I thoroughly enjoy rollerblading, ice-skating, walking the trail up Mt. Royal and best of all, miles of vigorous outdoor biking.

Poor listening skills are one of my ADD/H traits. Because it is often impossible to put aside my own racing thoughts and focus on someone else's words, I frequently interrupt whoever is speaking. When talking with someone, my verbal hyperactivity leaps from one topic to another.

There are times I can get lost when cycling in an unfamiliar neighborhood and must ask for directions. If the person gets too wordy, my ADD/H kicks in; I get antsy, unable to stay focused on the instructions; I will then break off the conversation, express my thanks, and speed away!

If angered by someone, my impulsive language gets me embroiled in a heated exchange - spewing forth vulgar words at the person who confronted me.

Speaking of verbal retorts, when I'm Food Shopping and dissatisfied with service at the check-out, my anger can burst forth with an insult aimed at the cashier: "If you give your tongue a rest and stop yakety-yaking with the customer, maybe you'll have time to ring up my groceries!" (See Chapter 10)

On a day when the workplace cafeteria menu is worse than usual, I make snide remarks for others to hear, such as: "The macaroni and cheese smells like unwashed feet." or "The sausage reminds me of dog sh*t."

The copy machine at work is frequently out of paper, toner, jammmed or otherwise not functioning. A line of people ahead of me will intensify my annoyance. In frustration, I might suggest we rent a bus to Quebec City, chain ourselves to the Parliament Building and refuse to budge until the government agrees to give us new equipment.

As a teenager living at home, ADD/H caused problems in taking care of my bedroom and its piles of clutter. Sometimes, with a burst of enthusiasm, I would begin a major cleanup of clothing, magazines and papers but soon gave it up, due to boredom and my pathetic organizing ability. Nothing has changed; any apartment I've lived in soon became an appalling mess! (See Chapter 20 - Executive Function Disorder)

Incapable of doing it alone, my supervisor at work periodically helps me organize my desk and work area.

On a happier note, one day, I found a dollar coin and treated myself to a pricey cup of frozen yogurt that I took home. I was about to scoop out a portion but stopped when a powerful impulse had me looking for a sleeping pill prescription, Dr. Freedman had given me. Since it was something important and fearing it was lost, I easily become unglued with frantic ADD/H behavior.

Sitting on the living room floor, my hunt for the prescription deteriorated into a frantic ransacking of my pocketbook and ripping apart the cloth partitions. During the search, I became even more distraught when realizing that a rain check from the supermarket was also missing. Much time was spent by repeated rummaging but with no success. It threw me into an out-of-control meltdown at war with my purse, dumping papers on the floor and flinging sundry objects across the room. (See Chapter 7 - Anxiety and Meltdowns) Eventually, with a sense of relief, I found the valued papers in a purse compartment, one that was rarely used.

Suddenly, recalling my frozen treat, I rushed to the kitchen and found the yogurt had become a container of "warm soup." My reaction was another meltdown; this time one of screaming and viciously biting my arms.

In retrospect, the two phases of meltdown rage were ADD hyperactive to the nth degree. By not doing the tasks in logical sequence, I reacted with poor executive function. Someone not hyperactive would have first enjoyed some frozen yogurt, then later do a proper search - not wild, but systematic!

I am prone to hyperactive outbursts. While out shopping on the day after 9/11, my bike frame was vandalized; it had been parked outdoors, attached to a metal post. Infuriated by the damage, I threw a hyperactive tantrum of stamping my feet, screaming bloody murder, punching my chest and biting my hands - all of this done in public. Sobbing, I walked the wreck to a nearby bicycle shop; then after much cajoling, the mechanic agreed to make the repairs when he finished the job he was doing. An hour later, feeling lots better, I was able to ride the bike home.

When feeling hyperactive and in a mood to be argumentative, I bait people by discussing problems that give me openings to shoot down whatever they suggest. For example, I will mention what could be an impossibly boring ten days of SARS quarantine, waiting for someone to suggest diversions like reading novels or watching TV sitcoms; both of which are perfect openings for me to sound-off on two intense dislikes that I consider worthless time-killers!

I have a decent job and don't allow ADD/H to adversely affect my final output of work. However, many days when overwhelmed with racing thoughts and external distractions, I keep slipping off task. I will find a job mentally exhausting, when forcing myself to stay focused on a piece of work, with a deadline that cannot wait.

As medical library assistant, I can do a <u>workaround</u>* to overcome difficulties presented by ADD/H. By living a few blocks from the nursing home, I can return in the evening, at a less hectic time, to accomplish what I could not focus on during the day.

Compared to <u>neurotypical</u>* people, I am hypersensitive to boredom. Pushing myself to do a *tedious* assignment can be sheer torture. To cope with monotony, I often divide an overall job into several parts, doing each one in sequence for 10 to 20 minutes - until arriving back at the first one. I then repeat the process until every segment gets done. It is an effective ADD/H workaround that breaks up the job, forestalling tedium and unrest.

Due to a singular trait of my autism - that overrides ADD/H - if I find a topic interesting, I take much pleasure in doing the fine detail that is required. A good example, that has me attentive and skilled, is intricate computer data processing, which I thoroughly enjoy!

CONCLUSION:
Attention deficit disorder/hyperactivity can tragically impact a person's life. For Marla, it is associated with workplace difficulties, homecare disorganization, emotional strife, and unsatisfactory interpersonal relations. Her hectic and sometimes frantic existence is due, in large part, to the ADD/H disorder.

The next chapter deals with Tourette syndrome, affecting Marla's entire life.

6

Tourette Syndrome

INTRODUCTION:
Prior to the 1960's, Tourette Syndrome (TS) was generally considered by physicians to be a <u>psychogenic</u>* behavioral disorder, treated by psychotherapy.

In the early 1960's, there was a growing realization that TS was not psychogenic but, in fact, a complex <u>neuro-psychiatric</u>* disorder; a condition of the nervous system characterized by involuntary movements and vocalizations referred to as tics.

Marla's TS disorder began in childhood. Her body tics included sudden twitches of the head, eye-blinks and grimacing, while her vocal tics consisted of sounds and words.

The tics would come and go, vary in intensity and change over time. They would be preceded by a strong urge to make the sound or do the movement; resisting the urge is perhaps best described as having to sneeze, while trying to hold it back.

Many individuals with TS are afflicted with a number of Co-morbid disorders that may include an attention deficit problem, compulsive behavior, a short temper, and low frustration tolerance. It is believed that TS adds to the severity of these behaviors, as is the case with Marla. (See Chapter 21)

In any event, both parents were convinced that Marla's tics were deliberate behaviors, she controlled at will!

Text:
When growing up, my vocal tics were coughs, barking, squeaks, gasping, clicking noises, repetitive language and frequent shifting from one sound to another.

The motor tics were also varied: stretching my mouth, blinking, shaking my head, putting a finger in my mouth, turning in circles and opening my eyes wide. During any particular time period, days or weeks, certain tics were dominant.

There were also temporary, situational tics triggered by noises, visual stimuli, or feelings.

Sometimes when a song I hated was played on the radio, symptomatic of TS, I would shriek with a high-pitched barking noise, mimicking the sound of an instrument playing the accompaniment.

During a time when my Vomiting Phobia was at its worst, over-and-over, I kept repeating the words *throw up*. (See Chapter 22)

Sometimes, I would do movement and noise tics in unison, such as head shaking and coughing simultaneously.

Although hating school, I unconsciously needed the structured routine, so that tics were usually worse if classes were not in session. Therefore, any excitement or break in the usual routine worsened my tics; even during pleasurable events, such as vacations, holidays and getting a present.

When I was playing outdoors, Mother watched me from the kitchen window and would call me inside when she saw me doing tics. Then, in a high-pitched voice, she would threaten to lock me in the basement if my *disgusting behavior* continued.

There were other threats. She said I would forever lose my voice if the "barking" continued or surely go blind if the blinking did not stop. It should be noted that because of having Autism, with a tendency to take threats literally, I believed her warnings and was terrified! (See Chapter 2)

When feeling the start of tics and fearful of either parent, I would seek refuge in my bedroom.

I remember times, sitting at the evening dinner table, when the tics were inevitable. Mother would humiliate me by attracting the family's attention to them.

While Father never threatened me with punishment, he had methods of embarrassing me. If he saw me shaking my head, he would exclaim with sarcasm, "I see you're doing the *shake* again." Or, he might ask, "What's that?" and then proceed to mimic, with exaggeration, whatever tic I was doing.

Years of my growing up in the 1950's and 1960's, our visits to a few doctors, because of the tics, were wasted efforts. I've since read that in those days most physicians thought the tics were no more than psychological reactions brought on by stress. (While tics are not *caused* by stress, my tic behaviors are more severe in effect when experiencing inordinate stress or tension.)

Since my parents were given false information that tics were psychological, I was increasingly pressured to stop doing them. If I insisted the tics were neurological, involuntary and beyond my control - as a few enlightened doctors believed - Mother would angrily exclaim, "There you go again, trying to invent a new illness!"

Even if they believed, as two doctors suggested, that my tics might be products of mental tension, it was no justification for their scolding and humiliation; they created even greater stress and made the spasms more pronounced.

Both parents were capable of feeling compassion for <u>NT</u>* people, including my two sisters. However, they had zilch sympathy for an anti-social daughter and were convinced that all of my atypical behaviors, including TS, could be restrained if I wished to do so.

As was the case with developmentally disabled children, growing up in the 1960's, there was no professional treatment for TS. But unlike me, countless others lucked-out by having tolerant parents.

By age 12, my TS acting *alone* was less frequent. Although, even as an adult, there are still singular remnants: I sometimes emit a squeaking, low-sounding vocal tic and do body tics that involve a tensing of muscles. When enduring a head cold, I have a tendency to utter gasping tic noises. Because of speech hesitancy, my words do not flow smoothly; there are short gaps in my voice caused by a series of muscle-tensing tics.

Now, as an adult, what has markedly increased is TS acting in tandem with other disorders - reinforcing and intensifying them. For example, TS acts in concert with my Passive-Aggressive Personality Disorder, so that when committing an act of vandalism, I also experience a feeling of TS relief, not dissimilar to the sensuality of ordinary tic relief. (See Chapter 33)

With TS acting in concert with Oppositional Defiant Disorder, I am more impulsive and aggressive than if I did an ODD behavior by itself. (See Chapter 27)

Some of my behavior in talking non-stop and not listening to others is caused by my Attention Deficit Disorder/Hyperactivity and a TS related lack of inhibition. I know it is rude to monopolize a conversation but frequently I cannot stop doing so. (See Chapter 5)

My TS also involves mimicking behaviors. These are involuntary "copycat" sounds and are made in response to kitchen *noises* that I find unnerving - such as objects pulled along the kitchen counter or falling in the sink. (See Chapter 19 - Synaesthesia, for other examples)

As a Touretter, I have a low frustration tolerance and break things when frustrated or overwhelmed - typical is my behavior in having wrecked more than one kitchen! (See Chapter 11 - Kitchen Chores)

CONCLUSION:

Nowadays, mental health professionals believe that TS is an incurable, inborn neurological disorder of the CNS <u>central nervous system</u>* . There is currently no medical test for clinically diagnosing TS.

As an adult, she rarely has tics acting alone, but does experience *tic traits* affecting and exacerbating her inattention, hyperactivity, distractibility, impulsivity, obsessions and mood swings.

Improvements will only happen if Marla relocates from Montreal to a small, amicable, less stressful city that better meets her needs for outdoor exercise and other advantages. By having a markedly *improved* lifestyle environment, it will be less likely to trigger the co-morbid disorders that now act in synergy with her TS.

The next chapter deals with interruptions and unexpected happenings in her daily routines. Marla may react with responses of screaming, biting, repetitive language and sometimes regression to childhood.

7

Anxiety and Emotional Meltdowns

INTRODUCTION:

Marla suffers from an anxiety disorder - a state of fear and apprehension pertaining to current situations and future events. When anxiety is acute and her usual routines are prevented, an emotional meltdown is often triggered that impedes physical and cognitive functioning, i.e. loss of reality, childish regression and gibberish talk - which can be ongoing until the crisis is over.

Text:

Constant anxiety is the most debilitating aspect of my autism because during every waking moment, relaxation is never possible. My central nervous system* is worn-out from stress and constant worry. (See Chapter 23 - Chronic Nervous Fatigue)

Just for starters, topics of worry include: coming down with a serious illness, my inevitable aging, and stranded with no support whenever Father is out of town. (See Chapter 4) Now, in his senior years his becoming ill or dying is a major source of my anxiety.

Other topics that bug me are crop failures, higher food prices, blackouts, foul weather preventing outdoor exercise, and unavailable car rides to Mt. Royal*. (See Chapter 12 - Exercise or Oblivion)

I also have intermittent worries about natural gas leaks, fire alarms, water main breaks, global warming, terrorism, weapons of mass destruction, and other manifestations of the Quickening. (See Chapter 34)

In the condo building where I live, any notice received from the business office creates anxiety even before reading it! Some notices turn out harmless; others conflict with my normal routines, such as a power shutdown needed for maintenance. Another notice might allude to costly repairs, requiring a surcharge which I can ill afford. But even more fundamental, there is an aspect of me that wants to be *left alone*; I've always hated the rules and regulations mandated by authority and want none of them; condo notices fall in that category!

I told Dr. Webster, my current psychiatrist, about a recent power outage and emotional meltdown. Suffering was extreme because the nerve calming pills, I ordinarily take for a blackout, did not function. He explained: "It was caused by a *digestive shutdown*; the medication you swallowed was not absorbed and remained undigested in your stomach until the crisis was over; a happening symptomatic of acute stress and anxiety."

Whenever I've phoned a supportive person willing to "talk me through a storm," I later remain with only a vague recollection of the actual meltdown and its cause; apparently, it has some kind of brain-numbing effect that prevents normal memory function.

Based on what others have reported about the meltdowns, I can only provide a rough idea of the weird "blah-blah" that tumbles out of my mouth. During extreme weather conditions, my speech becomes a hodge-podge of questions and repetitive statements. I might threaten to "pull the big guns," and swallow large doses of intoxicating potions! The gibberish might also include something like: "The world is dying because a planetary shift took place in 2000 and I've begun taking six Valium pills!" There may spew forth some vile language blasting Montreal, accompanied by my vocal mimicry of storm noises pounding on the window.

Out of touch with reality, there are certain meltdown questions I will ask over-and-over: "Will I be able to go outside tomorrow? What should I do if the power goes off? Will the streets be salted? Do you think the storm will ever end? What is the temperature right now? Will freezing rain become ordinary rain? Will I ever again be able to walk the mountain trail?" And so on.

In addition, irrationality triggers a type of pedantic talk common to people with HFA*. I may ask pompous questions, such as: "Tell me if, tomorrow, I should activate the eye-opening morning program or do you suggest I remain in slumber?" I might then lecture my listener on abstruse topics, like: "atmospheric shifts" and "chemistry states of matter."

With an emotional meltdown, if I finally contact my father on the phone, the conversation is very different from any usual one. For instance, if I tell him something is amiss with the weather, such as freezing rain; his response can make me even more distraught: "So what do you want me to do about it?" If he needles me by saying: "You won't be able to get out of the house for several days," I will feel suicidal and respond with kooky death wishes.

During another meltdown time when he says something encouraging like, "Tomorrow will be a better day," I will feel no calmer but appreciate his being supportive. Incidentally, the only way I can snap out of a meltdown is when the crisis situation is *over*.

I have nothing but hatred for the new millennium; it is assaulting me with many crises I've always feared. I'm being consumed with worry, like never before. Though I've always been prone to anxiety, it is more acute now that nations are in various stages of high alert, emergencies, nuclear threats, chaos, terrorism and genocide.

There is no antidote to counteract my worries. In the past, there were people I depended on to put my anxieties in perspective, and give me a less troublesome outlook; but they no longer live in Montreal. An even greater loss was my Psychiatrist, a pillar of support for over 30 years, who died in 2004. (See Chapter 14)

Nor does lively music provide any relaxation or relief from my anxiety. The kinds of songs I enjoy can be stimulating but the worries still remain; sleep is my *only* temporary relief.

For me, the Quickening aspects most fearful are those with the potential to disrupt my daily routines.

All I get from the current crop of acquaintances, in the workplace, are trite remarks, such as: "We should not worry about a disaster hitting Montreal until it happens," or "The media tend to exaggerate because sensationalism is good for business," and "Most any crisis we hear about should be taken with a grain of salt." These kinds of stereotypical platitudes can never lessen my anxiety.

CONCLUSION:
Due to severe autism, Marla lacks the innate ability to put life's potential crises and worries on the back burner. Problems in her personal life plus potential crises of non-compliance with daily routines are what trouble her the most. Since she cannot be talked out of what *may* happen, the best anyone can do is offer modified, somewhat less troubling perspectives.

To her parents' credit, they were concerned about Marla's inability to relax. As noted in the next chapter, they supported the idea of her undergoing Transcendental Meditation.

8

Meditation and Relaxation

INTRODUCTION:
All her life, Marla has suffered from unrelenting stress and tension. Conscious relaxation has never been possible. In varying degrees, it is a condition that occupies and often dominates every waking moment. Deep sleep is her only respite.

Text:
At age 15, I was going through rough times with my family and the teachers at school. I needed the antidote of frequently talking with someone who would be understanding and verbally supportive; the weekly, one hour session with my psychiatrist was hardly enough. (See Chapter 14 - Psychiatrist)

Meandering downtown, I often browsed in book stores and record shops. One day, I walked into the storefront of a religious cult that served free coffee. Approached by a member who welcomed me, she explained some basics of their Jesus cult*. By mentioning my problems with tenseness and stress, I was shown some Bible passages and told that its teachings would calm my nerves.

I felt accepted by the group and began showing up most days, drinking their coffee and talking with members who were friendly.

My fling with the Jesus people was partly rooted in my need for emotional support. Conditions had worsened at home and there were daily fights with my parents. Pouring my heart out to members of the sect was comforting while I sipped their free beverages.

Though I may have been seeking "a new family," the attraction was more than that. Unable to calm my nerves, I was hoping their religion would teach me how to do it. It was a cult whose teachings were based on a mystical version of Christianity that I found appealing.

I also found myself looking for proof that God existed and thumbed through the Bible searching for tangible instructions on how to *contact* Him; all the while beseeching Him to answer my prayers.

For two important reasons, I finally gave up on the cult's teachings. After almost a year of orientation, I could neither make contact with God nor learn the cult's techniques for relaxing my nerves. Since my autism prevents any social feeling, the members' friendship was no inducement to continue. (See Chapter 2 - Autism)

Some months later, I turned to transcendental meditation, a mental technique to promote relaxation, reduce stress and improve one's quality of life. It all began when my parents and I responded to an advertisement for a free TM lecture meeting.

TM sounded promising. I was subsequently enrolled in the program which advocated a technique of meditation, derived from Hindu traditions and said to promote deep relaxation. We were hopeful that with meditation, I would learn how to calm my nerves.

In addition, since too much eating is often related to stress and since I was overweight with a voracious appetite, Mother believed that if TM proved successful, my appetite would no doubt lessen.

Although TM is based on a religion, one originating in India, students are not required to adopt any spiritual beliefs. I had the option of learning just the meditation techniques for promoting deep relaxation. The TM is fulfilled through the use of a mantra; a word or phrase repeated over-and-over.

Sad to say, nothing was gained from studying TM. Due to having an Attention Deficit Disorder, I could not prevent my mind from wandering. It was impossible to clear my consciousness and remain focused on the mantra - repeating it for twenty minutes! Whenever I became sleepy and dozed off, it was the only time meditation relaxed me! (See Chapter 5)

My parents, who were paying for the TM lessons, were on a constant lookout for signs of improvement, yet saw none! For their investment, they had anticipated much more than my goal of conscious relaxation. On one occasion, Mother said that TM was no good because I remained overweight with a huge appetite and still wore oversized dresses!

Another time in high school, I brought home a mediocre report card. There were high marks in math, yet barely passing grades in other subjects. During a confrontation at the dinner table and seeing my deplorable grade point average, it reinforced Mother's belief that TM was of no value!

Shortly thereafter, at age 17, due to hormone problems, I had a day of heavy menstrual bleeding, characterized by hysteria. Because I was unable to calmly deal with the bleeding, Mother's low opinion of TM was reinforced. In short, the program got blamed for virtually every defect in my functioning ability.

Because of my ineptitude in doing the mantra, *for that reason alone,* I quit TM after 18 months of wasted effort.

CONCLUSION:

All her life, Marla has been trying, without success, to achieve conscious relaxation.

In time, it became obvious to her that one needed an ability to sufficiently *let go of racing thoughts,* in order for religion or transcendental meditation to succeed in eliminating stress.

Other than the normal night's sleep, the only way Marla can relax her mind is by *unconscious* relaxation, namely deep sleep, available on demand with sleeping pills and booze. (See Chapter 12 - Exercise or Oblivion)

In the next chapter, Marla verbally attacks the Montreal environment and its harsh climate.

9

Montreal and Climate

INTRODUCTION:
Marla was born and raised in Montreal, Canada. As an adult with multiple neurological disorders, it has become increasingly difficult to survive in the mainstream of a mobbed city, a cacophony of languages, a pervasive rudeness and an atrocious climate. The city's inclement weather thwarts Marla's need for daily, outdoor biking.

Text:
Montreal is an irritant to my nervous system. There are traffic jams, broken glass, reckless drivers, endless road construction, stores packed with people, and put downs for my Anglo heritage. Since I don't speak the language, the French majority has no use for me.

None of the mental health professionals, I'm aware of, except Drs. <u>Amitta Shah</u>* and <u>Christopher Gillberg</u>* acknowledge the negative effects that an environment can have on a person with autism.

People in my circle expect me to stop complaining about Montreal and learn to cope. Impossible! The environment is so abrasive I could never adjust to it; with constant reminders of inadequate public service, a city administration wracked by austerity and a dolittle municipal workforce. While in desperate need of daily home care, CLSC* Montreal social services gives me nothing but one inadequate hour per week.

Since the passing of Dr. Freedman, the weekly session I now have is with the only psychiatrist who had an opening. His basic philosophy that people can accomplish most anything, if they only set their mind to it, is patently ridiculous. It is neither consistent with my severe neuro-disorders* that are hardwired and immutable to change, nor is he providing the supportive counseling that I desperately need. (See Chapter 14 - Psychiatrist)

Montreal is racked with frantic, nervous activity and gridlock traffic, seven days a week. Living among a profusion of mean, uncaring, people brings out my venomous dark side - fueling my own rudeness, hostility and Oppositional behavior. (See Chapter 27)

Every season has countless bad weather days that keep me housebound. Winter is the worst! It becomes a season of unrelenting misery with countless days of no exercise possible. As a victim of cabin fever - confined to my apartment - I suffer from boredom, restlessness and irritability. I then must blot out the anguish with pills and booze consigning me to Oblivion. (See Chapter 12)

The winter climate is so violent; it defies all attempts to dress for the weather. The onslaught of rain, snow and fierce winds penetrate everything I wear. By rendering umbrellas worthless, their twisted remains are strewn everywhere.

When biking is not possible during the cold months, climbing the mountain trail is sometimes an option. Ironically, when I have the greatest need for a car ride to Mt. Royal, the JFS* Jewish Family Services volunteer drivers "cease to exist." As snowbird retirees, they jet to Florida for the winter while I remain stranded with no means of transportation except for my father, if and when, he happens to be available.

As for rollerblading in the Butler Building, there are problems. First of all, Butler is not a true building because of its two sides, south and east, that are without walls. When the weather is unfit for biking, it is often not feasible to skate on concrete that is wet or icy. Even during good weather, there is usually enough slippery garbage and broken glass on the surface to risk a mishap when rollerblading. At times, when Butler gets monopolized by teenagers skating wildly, so as not to get mauled by them, I'm forced to vacate the place in a mood of angry frustration.

For the neighborhood ice rink, my best skating occurs from late March through late May, because all the regular bookings are finished for the season and the secretary often lets me on the ice, early in the day. The only bad sessions are when aggressive teenagers get on the ice, begin to race around, and monopolize the rink; then I have no choice but to quit the session and go home in tears!

Montreal is a wild scene! The city's tempo accelerates as people rush from place-to-place. Dyspraxia is the cause of my relatively slow response time. Not quick enough to avoid people's sudden movements, I can easily bump into them - in a congested store, biking on a busy street, or skating among young people. (See Chapter 17)

I've noticed a pervasive lack of kindness and civility in the Montreal police department. One day in approaching my street, police cars were rushing past. My worst fear became a reality seeing that my high-rise building was indeed their destination. There were five police cars and an ambulance, with attendants lifting an injured man from the ground onto a stretcher.

Remembering 9/11, I feared a terrorist attack. The greatest concern was being deprived of my routines. Anticipating no supper, no time at the computer, and not sleeping in my bed - I had an emotional meltdown asking officers where I'd be able to spend the night; I was either ignored, given vague answers or told they didn't know!

Sheer terror gripped me when a cop told someone that the area around the building was a crime scene. At that point, my brain seemingly collapsed, and feeling like a two year old I began asking officers if it was safe to go inside and "make a pee pee." One cop shouted, "Get the hell away before you do it in front of me!"

A short time later, with the emergency over, we were allowed into the building and my Emotional Meltdown instantly vanished. (See Chapter 7)

My fear of a terrorist attack was unfounded but what did occur affected me deeply. A middle-aged man with a history of mental illness had jumped off his 4th floor balcony, was critically injured and later died in the hospital.

Besides rude cops, the city has a labor force of blue-collar workers protected by powerful unions. Knowing they cannot be fired, the goof-offs are lethargic and do shoddy work.

Threats of strikes against the government and actual walkouts are chronic problems. Unions that most affect me are garbage collection, electric power, the nursing home where I work and also the ice skating rink. While the negotiations are in progress, I suffer from months of uncertainty. If the walkout occurs, I become a nervous wreck due to cut-off services, interfering with my daily routine.

Over the years, several support people in my life, who meant a great deal to me, have relocated. Some were forced to leave the province because they could not pass the French language test; now a Quebec government requirement to qualify for most employment. They've been replaced by disadvantaged, non-English speaking immigrants from third world French-speaking countries - flocking to Montreal in droves.

Foreign languages are not my forte and I've resisted learning to speak French. Inasmuch as I began working in the nursing home before the French language requirement became law, I am exempt from the regulation. However, if I quit the job or were terminated, my French exemption would be null and void. And except for unskilled, menial work, I would not qualify for new employment in Quebec.

Living in a city where English is fast becoming a "second language," I have problems communicating with several co-workers and people in all walks of life.

Due to the political uncertainties surrounding the <u>Quebec separatism</u>* movement, I feel insecure about the future. I have no wish to live in a province that speaks a different language and where the majority are antagonistic toward someone speaking English.

Not conversant in French, there is also potential danger. During a yearly bike race in progress, I was waiting to cross the street while the officer directing traffic spoke in French. Thinking that pedestrians were told to proceed, I mistakenly began walking my bike across the intersection. Suddenly, to avoid getting hit by a car missing me by inches, I jumped out of the way! Not understanding French in this city can be risky business!

The roads are deplorable with numerous potholes and other disrepair; streets are prevalent with broken glass and all manner of trash. Biking in this city is also hazardous due to gridlock traffic, blockage at key intersections, and French traffic signs without English translations.

As much as I enjoy biking, I breathe a sigh of relief when returning home safely - with my bike and tires undamaged - having avoided numerous potholes and broken glass. In addition, I'm no longer subjected to road rage and motorists cursing me with foul language.

I avoid Montreal bike paths since they are too narrow, dangerously overcrowded and loaded with filth - due to poor maintenance.

Even the city's music is worthless. Since the 1990's, sorrowful songs are embraced by Montreal's French culture. The summer, outdoor festivals of lively music are either gone or replaced by depressing, melancholy ballads. Radio stations no longer play upbeat music; it's either talk-radio or whining love songs. Soulful, lamenting music coming from loudspeakers in supermarkets and the creepy ballads outpouring from car radios remind me that I live in a joyless city - forlorn of all hope - playing sounds of music that belong in a funeral parlor!

Visitors can be fooled by the artificial hospitality shown by hotel staff and the salespeople in fashion boutiques. Tourists are lured by the fast pace, French ambience, restaurants, hotels, bars, night clubs, prostitutes, strip joints and sporting events. Most of the attractions that lure visitors to Montreal, I find repulsive; those amusements do little, or nothing, to improve the quality of life for people who live here.

Even worse than the saccharine music and tourist traps is a climate that takes everything out of me. So much mental energy is consumed in dealing with the weather, there is not much left to accomplish anything productive. With bad weather ongoing or expected, I'm in a foul mood and find it difficult to act civilly toward anyone.

Before the five months of winter weather set in, fall days in Montreal get inundated with steady rain and cold temperature. It's not even the weather per se that *psychs me out* but that I'm prevented from biking. As an alternate workout, rollerblading in the Butler Building or a walk on the mountain trail is sometimes possible. If none of these are feasible, sleeping pills, booze and Oblivion are my only recourse. (See Chapter 12)

People suggest that during bad weather, I do an hour of vigorous walking in the nearby, enclosed shopping mall - a substitution I always shoot down; making it clear that I must have a vigorous walk, such as an uphill climb on the <u>Mt. Royal</u>* trail; whereas walking on a flat surface is relatively worthless.

In Montreal, I cannot depend on having good weather even in late spring. Bitterly cold conditions in June often have vegetable crops dying of frost. No biking and a ruined vegetable crop disallow two vital components in my lifestyle - exercise and affordable produce. Once on a spring day, when a radio newscast predicted this *double whammy*, my reaction was to lie face down on the bed and cry for hours!

With global warming, we often have violent thunderstorms during June and July. When bad weather and no exercise have me housebound and feeling bloated, it's like a heavy weight on my chest and my stomach loaded with super-glue.

I recall, October 2002, when winter had roared in unexpectedly and for three consecutive days, we were locked in a cold, windy, wet system with ice pellets coming down in the afternoon and snow during the night. It meant days of <u>cabin fever</u>*, as though January had arrived a season early. I kept wishing there was someone who would put me to sleep - with sedation - for the next several months, until spring!

As a partial healing process, I need lots of good summer weather to compensate for the cabin fever and oblivion of fall-winter. But I know from past experience, the curative power of summer is nothing I can depend on. I'm reminded of the incessant rain, during July and August of 2002, that made biking outdoors or walking the mountain trail an impossible dream.

Most of summer has me sweltering in humidity and awaiting the next lightning storm! Entire summers, during this millennium had, at most, three or four weeks of good weather. I've then forced to withstand the bitter months of fall/winter, though lacking sufficient physical and mental recuperation from summer.

Media weather reports have been the bane of my life. If the following weeks forecast calls for a stretch of bad weather, I become increasingly agitated and dread each passing day. If good weather is predicted and I feel hopeful, a change for the worse, in an updated forecast, throws me into a state of <u>situational depression</u>*. Therefore, I no longer consult long range forecasts; they are too unreliable.

Because a thunder and lightning storm can result in a blackout, there is always fear of losing electric power; the result would be an interruption of the routines that keep my life functioning. Should that occur, I will have an emotional meltdown that requires a caring person to talk me through the ordeal with kind words and verbal support. In non-supportive Montreal, I don't know of such a person!

When telephoning Mother in a state of panic, during an exceptionally bad winter storm, in 1999, I will never forget her distraught tone of voice saying I should be "put away" during the cold weather.

She vowed to never again let me burden her with another winter of my anxiety; in future years, she and Father would vacation in Florida. It was made clear they were sick to death of hearing my fear of nobody available for rides to the mountain or take me grocery shopping. They were determined to follow my psychiatrist's advice of living their own lives, and letting me fend for myself.

In the midst of having an emotional meltdown, instead of telephoning Mother, I once made the mistake of going there; a fight soon erupted and Mother - out of control - began shrieking at me. Talking on the phone or going there made no difference; either way, I received a tongue-lashing. In this case, it was for having a panic attack of no less than a combination of windstorm, freezing rain and pellets of hail!

One day, Mother and I made future plans for a mountain walk; sadly the day turned out miserable and a freezing rain made our plans impossible. When telephoning her and despondent in a *blue funk*, my voice was in a state of panic - bordering on meltdown. I cried out asking if the rain would ever stop! She reacted with her edgy tone of voice that I knew was anger directed at me, for being so upset. With the mountain walk cancelled, stymied, nowhere to turn and in a burst of rage I smashed the phone and everything breakable in the living room!

Since it can cause a power outage, it is one reason I fear the on-slaught of freezing rain. Once the freeze begins, neither my father nor JFS* people will drive on slick roads. Even if the trip isn't cancelled, a trip to the mountain often serves no purpose, when the walking trail had become a sheet of ice. With tears of disappointment, I'm forced to return home!

For several winters, with high frequency, we've had freezing rain storms and blizzard conditions. I might add that each Montreal winter of suffering adds a layer of stress to my central nervous system.

People think that after several hated ice storms, I'd get used to them and they'd be less stressful. It has never happened that way; each freezing rain affects me as a new and distinct crisis.

My dislike of Montreal includes repugnance for most people that I've encountered. My rotten upbringing plus an Autism disorder have laid the foundation for my negative attitude toward humanity. It's impossible to develop positive feelings for people when I'm bombarded with rudeness and hostility. My only chance for having a good life is relocation, out of here, to a small city with a good climate and civilized people. (See Chapter 2)

When I advise a student visiting the library to relocate out of Montreal, it is not meant as a friendly gesture. Frankly, I have no interest in the student's future; it is advice strictly motivated by a feel-good emotion when expressing my hatred of Montreal!

Montreal is unsafe and filthy. All one has to do is go for a ride on our streets to see the garbage, broken glass and potholes that abound. People here delight in smashing bottles and treating the streets like garbage dumps. When biking on many of the thoroughfares, the stench is unbearable! City workers are too busy goofing off to adequately clean the streets and repair dangerous potholes. Supposedly on the job, they may be seen noshing in a donut shop or having a snooze in their vehicle.

I have to admit that Montreal brings out the worst in me and negatively affects my demeanor; I have no interest in being productive and spend much of my waking time rebelling! (See Chapter 33 - Passive Aggressive Disorder)

My California pen-pal told me that any person, including the most stable NT*, can descend into irrationality if subjected to enough stress. The living situation, in this wretched city, is now so bad that my acting-out with irrational behavior can be expected and does occur. An abusive upbringing began my ruination, while adult life in Montreal is the culmination of my downfall.

CONCLUSION:
For Marla, Montreal is the wrong environment; one reason is the horrendous climate that most of the year prevents outdoor exercise and keeps her housebound.

With multiple neurological disorders, Marla finds it increasingly difficult to survive in the mainstream of an abrasive city. Since the government is overwrought by inefficiency, austerity and shrinking budgets she receives no social services and with Dr. Freedman's passing, the intermittent psychiatric counseling she now gets is grossly inadequate.

The next chapter is about food shopping in Montreal. Marla talks about the exorbitant prices charged for low-calorie food items; while all manner of junk food is frequently on special.

10

Food Shopping

INTRODUCTION:
As a youngster, Marla had a ravenous appetite for the family's home-cooked meals - high in fat and sugar. Throughout her childhood and teens she was considerably overweight. By age 19, she was determined to slim down with a combination of low calorie food and vigorous Exercise. (See Chapter 12)

A sensible diet that allows most foods to be eaten, but in moderation, would not provide the *bulk* that Marla desired. When she sits down to a meal, there is a craving for *inner fullness*. To prevent obesity, it had to be low calorie food in sufficient amounts to feel satisfied. As a result, Marla is an enthusiast of fresh vegetables and low-fat dairy products. This bulk diet satisfies her appetite, while the low-calories and daily exercise control her weight. To her credit, Marla has never deviated from this healthful routine.

Text:
Hardly a day goes by without my having a run-in with store personnel; their attitude toward me can be negative and even belligerent. For example, I recently had a miserable shopping day.

The grocery store had a cart filled with marked-downs, and I spent considerable time rummaging for items of use to me. Finally, I located a batch of Crystal Light diet drink packets, but without the reduced prices attached.

When I inquired, an employee told me that only the manager, who was off that day, had the authority to set prices on marked-down items. I became furious and told him that without the head honcho to make decisions, the store should go out of business. I then went to the checkout and was told by the cashier that the drinks were regular price, and were put in the discount cart by mistake. That was a blatant lie because the boxes containing the packets were damaged. I held back from calling the girl a moron but told her that she and the other employee were thieves and belonged in jail!

Not long ago, I visited an open-air food market which periodically gets infested with bees attracted by the fragrant fruits and vegetables on display. Terrified of being stung, I was hardly able to continue shopping.

I remarked to a nearby truck driver they should spray insecticide to get rid of the bees. Mocking me, he angrily retorted: "What do you think we are, exterminators?" He then exclaimed: "Bees are creatures of God with as much right to live as you do!" During the rest of my time at the market, whenever catching sight of me, he would holler snide remarks ridiculing my fear of bees.

Adding to my shopping misery, the storekeepers can be a nasty bunch. Early one day, I biked to the same outdoor market and saw nothing worthwhile at a price I could afford. A nearby food store, which sometimes had reasonably priced items, was closed. When I asked a manager in the adjacent booth what time the other place opened, he spewed forth a cacophony of French verbiage that I could little understand; I then suggested he speak English. In a belligerent tone of voice, he exclaimed, "Me speak no English!" His angry response, along with the stress of not finding any food, caused me to lose my temper; I retorted: "You are nothing but a French pig!" I knew it was wrong to react that way but frankly I was angry and didn't care. He retaliated by hollering remarks about the "dirty English." Although I expressed my insult only once, he repeated "dirty English" over-and-over, screaming so loud I could still hear him a block away!

In another store, low fat ice cream was missing from the shelf. I was told that the product was now off the market, as was the sugar free, low-fat yogurt. Hearing the bad news, devastating to my food routine, puts me in a sour mood, with a wish to vandalize the whole store!

In summer, I can put some fruits and vegetables on the table, but affordable, low-fat dairy products - cottage cheese, yogurt and ice cream are little more than a memory. Low-income people, like me, can no longer afford healthful dairy foods.

The trend has been for local dairy companies to merge and thereby avoid price competition. I cannot afford high-protein, low-calorie foods at their current prices. One day, after visiting several stores and not finding a single dairy product within my budget, I rode the bike home in a state of anger, with tears streaming down my face!

Cottage cheese is never on special and the only cheese ever sold at a reduced price is Kraft processed slices, loaded with chemicals, that I refuse to eat. A low fat variety of cheddar cheese, I always depended on, has been discontinued.

I'm told that hundreds of new products are brought to market each year and since shelf space is limited, the slow-movers are discontinued and replaced by new items. This accounts for some of the products I must have but are no longer available.

Only the high fat, sugar laden yogurt is sometimes reduced in price; just seeing it on the shelf puts me in a vandalizing mood. Chocolate milk - one of the few dairy products occasionally on special - is chock-full of sugar and should be on display in the junk food section, where it belongs.

Years ago, when I could get marked down low-fat cottage cheese and yogurt with *past* expiration dates, I would buy up to 10 containers at a time and freeze them. The products were still good because yogurt and cottage cheese will stay fresh weeks longer, since their high acid content discourages growth of harmful bacteria. Bargains like that have disappeared. Beginning in the 1990's, fresh produce and low-fat dairy products have been either difficult to obtain or unaffordable. No longer are items with lapsed expiration dates sold at a discount.

During the fall, I can sometimes find fresh produce on special or marked down. I then suffer through the agonies of Dyspraxia in preparing vegetables for the freezer - washing, cutting and bagging all of the portions. I load the freezer to capacity with items like cauliflower, broccoli, green beans, Brussels sprouts and cabbage that will tide me through the early winter months. (See Chapter 17)

Because of erratic Quebec weather, there are years when fruits and vegetables cannot be grown locally. Outrageously expensive produce is then imported from other countries. The pricey imports put me in a frenzied mood to stock up on whatever locally grown ones are still available.

By mid-winter, there are problems when I need to replenish some of the food items; weather conditions are fraught with blizzards and icy conditions so that biking is impossible. I'm stuck with nowhere to shop but at a pricey food store in the nearby mall. The products so expensive and the employees so rude, I'd like to see the entire shopping complex gutted, and made into a rollerblade rink!

The chain supermarkets are clean and well stocked but with food prices so high that low income people cannot afford them.

In past years, I was permitted to take leftover vegetables from the nursing home where I work - a benefit that is no longer allowed. Another plus, now gone, are mom and pop stores within walking distance, selling overripe or slightly blemished produce at reduced prices. I also depended on seconds, with imperfections, by scavenging the dumpster behind a store near my workplace. These days, seconds are rarely available in stores and are not to be had in a dumpster that is kept locked.

Since the late nineties, the few markdowns being sold are either in a store going bankrupt or a worthwhile product being discontinued. While I enjoy the closeout sale price, knowing the item will no longer be available can upset me a great deal.

In this millennium of inflated food prices what follows are two, once in a blue moon, shopping surprises:

I took a long bike ride to a grocery store that offered occasional specials. To my astonishment, they had sixty boxes of flavored diet-gelatin on the markdown shelf, at a bargain price of twenty-nine cents each. I felt proud of myself for apparently being the first shopper to find them. It was such a good buy I cleaned off the entire shelf and came home with all sixty boxes! The non-perishable gelatin powder can be stored for ages and I use it as a satisfying low-calorie snack.

By driving their cars everywhere, people are sedentary and increasingly obese. I've avoided that trap. In spring and summer, I cycle countless miles to get bargains and if I find some it requires considerable exercise-energy, lugging them home in my backpack. During a long bike ride, I visited a variety store and noticed a basket of assorted snacks being sold at a discount. Most of the items were sugary junk but with some effort, I not only fished out six packages of diet candies, at a good markdown, but to my pleasant surprise also a bunch of loose dimes; I considered it a payback for the outrageous 15% Quebec sales tax - good luck that I delighted in!

Despite the few good times mentioned, annoying problems are the usual occurrence. When in a store and need assistance to find a product, I can ask for help but hesitate because it leads to arguments. I lack the pragmatic skills needed to get a clerk's cooperation. (Pragmatics can be defined as the social use of language, a skill that allows people to express themselves in ways that are likely to get a positive response.) It is a skill that I often lack because my negative emotions hinder or prevent it. For instance, in seeking assistance, I always anticipate being disappointed, either not locating the product or one that is too costly.

Dissatisfaction with food shopping can provoke rudeness toward a clerk who is trying to help me find something, but is having no success. I might belittle him with the announcement: "I don't have all day!"

Many newcomers from other countries take low-wage jobs in our retail stores. By me having zilch ability with foreign languages, my grocery shopping can be torturous. Few of these employees know anything and those who do cannot "speekie de Englis."

When I am able to buy something, I usually get irritated by a long, slow checkout line. Then under my breath or to someone next to me, I mumble some choice obscenities about the city and its lackadaisical workers. On the most stressful days, I directly bad mouth the cashier as a "sleeping beauty" or a "work-shy person." If the line is held up by her yakking with someone, I might holler: "Less social cackling will get more work done!"

If product labels are in English, stores are required, by Quebec statute, to affix them with French language versions. The sticker will frequently conceal the all-important nutrition information as to calories, sugar, fat, sodium, etc. It is a careless practice threatening my health and that of others, who must limit our intake of harmful nutrients.

Much of my food shopping consists of disappointments that inspire vandalism. Often, there is no affordable produce except limes, bananas, and mangoes - for which I have no use! I often walk out of a store, having accomplished nothing but acts of vandalism. When foods are overpriced with nothing affordable, I feel the urge to trash every junk food item in the place! (See Chapter 33 - Passive Aggressive)

I have a gripe with most people's food preferences in Montreal; namely their love affair with unhealthy, fattening slop. I happen to be affected, since these people cut off demand for low-calorie food, increasingly difficult to find and rarely on special.

In contrast, junk foods abound in every supermarket and get advertised to the limit with hefty discounts. Also, in the nursing home where I work, the cafeteria menu specializes in pig food. Since the swill is acceptable to a majority of patrons, my requests for serving healthy food get ignored!

I sometimes envision finding a pill to restrain my voracious appetite and then go on a public hunger strike, protesting Montreal's abysmal food situation.

CONCLUSION:
In all the years we've corresponded, Marla's food circumstances have never been this bleak. The poor availability of healthful products, along with outrageous prices, play havoc with her food routine.

Chapter 11 will next discuss Marla's evening meal routine fraught with suffering and self-abuse.

11

Kitchen Chores and Self-Abuse

INTRODUCTION:
For Marla, kitchen chores are loathsome and accompanied by intense anger. From the time she was first told to help out in the kitchen, at age seven, it has been a hateful experience. At home and then later, as an adult in her own apartment, she would chew on a worktable and vent her rage by damaging the kitchen cabinets - all the while struggling to do food preparation. Now, later in life, to forestall kitchen damage in her upscale apartment, Marla does not attack the kitchen, but discharges her rage with self-abuse.

Text:
Compared to other kinds of work, I notice my short term memory is worse when doing kitchen chores, i.e. remembering where I put the rags, scouring powder and utensils.

My arms - disfigured with sores and scabs - are proof-positive of my struggle in the kitchen. By the time I've prepared supper, the wounds are at their worst. If color photos were taken after a biting episode, my arms would show fresh blood in several places and scabs from the previous day. Limited by the amount of pain I can tolerate, I'm prevented from doing even worse damage to myself!

While kitchen work provokes my self-abuse, it becomes more intense if I've had a stressful day.

Kitchen meltdowns are not limited to the evening meal. At any time of day, if I've caused a kitchen mess, my teeth will go on the offensive.

Recently, during mid-day, I had an emotional meltdown. Both arms received an onslaught of biting; the result of having to do a major cleanup job. It was caused by trying to remove the pull-off tab from a can of soda and having splattered sticky liquid all over the kitchen.

In my earlier apartments, I made similar messes with difficult cleanups and experienced the same need to release anger. However, in those days, I would not inflict bodily abuse, but would vent anger by wrecking the kitchen. It would start with biting the counter tops and then inflicting additional damage, wherever possible.

Dr. Freedman suggested that when preparing a meal, I take a time-out whenever there is a build-up of anger. I rejected his idea, since the meal preparation has to get done; so even if I took a brief intermission, the chores would still be the same "angry beasts" when I returned. (See Chapter 14 - Psychiatrist)

In 1978, I lost my house key so that the super had to change the lock and give me a new key. He noticed that my kitchen had been demolished and reported it to the landlord who then notified my mother. In a fit of anger, she accused me of being mentally ill and said the only option remaining was to have me committed to the Douglas - Montreal's notorious mental institution!

The Douglas threat was said in anger by a mother in denial I had neurological disorders; she firmly believed that my wrecking behavior was controllable and done willfully. Though nothing ever came of her bluster, I was terrified nevertheless!

The landlord considered getting me thrown out of the apartment, but since I paid for the repairs, it seemed to settle the matter.

However, he made it clear, I could expect periodic inspections and an eviction notice, if there was any more damage.

I tried to restrain myself, but the resolve faded in a couple of days with the breakage continuing. Then a new landlord purchased the building, who kept it only a few months, and the place was sold again. In fact, the turnover was frequent and no owner was there long enough to bother getting on my case.

(As noted in the Introduction, when I later moved into a decent condo, the kitchen damage was replaced by self-abuse.)

While biting my arms, powerful emotions are inflicting multiple wounds. In the heat of rage, I temporarily lose touch with reality and am not troubled by the sight of blood. Later, however, aware of the unsightly sores and probable damage done to my arms and teeth, I have feelings of remorse.

Smashing kitchens and biting behavior are due to a low frustration tolerance, symptomatic of Tourette Syndrome. It is a neurological disorder in which hyperactivity, uncontrollable impulses and compulsivity get expressed; and, in my case, translated into a build-up of anger that must be vented. (See Chapter 6)

Besides the kitchen chores, there can be a cluster of events causing additional mental tension. I recall a morning of unusual stress that included: pressure at work, a rain storm, low on food, much thunder, and powerful winds - awful weather later imprisoning me at home. Those negatives, acting in synergy, resulted in a Meltdown of biting my arms and severe bleeding. (See Chapter 7)

In addition to biting behavior, I make strange noises! I hiss and scream, sometimes stomping and jumping. I also mimic irritating sounds in the kitchen; these occur when utensils touch each other; for instance, a spoon is stirred on a dish, a knife slides in the sink, or a utensil falls on the floor. While biting my arms, I vocalize the kitchen sounds until they become a close match to the ones irritating me. The intense hatreds of kitchen textures and sounds are caused by Sensory IIntegration Disorder - fueling the rages, anger arising from frustration and sensory irritation, I can offer no semblance of logic to explain behaviors that are purely physical, emotional and in no way thoughtful. (See Chapter 18)

After being rid of the daily chores and feeling a sense of relief, I leave the dirty dishes, soaking in the sink, to be tackled the following day. I don't do anything demanding after I eat dinner; it is mostly a time of quiet reading, crosswords, the Internet and other relaxation. Although the rages have stopped, the irritation lingers on with residue brain fatigue, impaired concentration and weakened short term memory.

Now that I'm living in a new condo, I want to keep the place in good condition. To discharge anger and frustration, the attack on my arms serves as the only outlet. Yet, my psychiatrist had suggested I go back to smashing up the kitchen, which he considered preferable to hurting myself. Since he was well-off financially, he lacked empathy for my weak earning ability; and by living at the poverty level, I cannot afford to have any more kitchens repaired.

The only solution for my self-abuse is to get relieved from doing kitchen chores. I need a housekeeper for at least one hour every day, but financially I cannot hack it. All <u>CLSC</u>* will provide is a measly one hour per week! What amounts to a trifle is due to their austerity budget plus a lack of interest in my case.

As with the vast majority of mental health professionals, the CLSC is hooked on the idea of the client doing self-improvement, as opposed to receiving supportive services. Not understood by this agency is that the disorders causing my kitchen crisis are hardwired, inborn and not amenable to change; they are the result of having several dysfunctional brain areas. (See Chapter 16 - Behavior Modification)

Because of my disabled hand-eye coordination, kitchen help is a must. Preparing fresh produce is an ordeal of being stuck with hours of cutting vegetables, cooking them and cleaning up the inevitable messes all over the kitchen. (See Chapter 17 - Dyspraxia)

Yet, if I'm not able to find affordable fresh vegetables, I'm distraught by not having enough proper food on hand. Either way, it's an impossible situation!

If I try to suppress the kitchen rage, I will later release the anger by doubly chewing my arms. A similar reaction occurs with Tourette Syndrome when I'm trying to hold the tics in. For example, in the workplace I may temporarily suppress the urge to tic but later, by myself at home, I'm forced to tic twice as much! (See Chapter 6)

As for the kitchen work itself, I think my difficulties go beyond bad hand coordination and poor sensory integration. Admittedly, I am also missing the <u>skill set</u>* needed to efficiently perform kitchen chores. These skills involve not only hand dexterity and the physical senses but also organization, sequences of movements, short term memory and spatial awareness. (See Chapter 20 - Executive Function)

It is obvious, I was never meant to do much with my hands and frankly I'm worn out from the struggle. My need is for someone to do many of my dexterity chores. I don't expect help in getting dressed or undressed but I desperately need assistance with the kitchen work and help in organizing the apartment clutter.

CONCLUSION:
As someone with severe autism and multiple Co-morbid disorders, life's chores frustrate Marla in varying degrees. However, nothing compares with the horror of rages, destruction, and self-mutilation when doing kitchen chores. (See Chapter 21)

The next chapter deals with the critical importance of daily exercise in Marla's life.

12

Exercise or Oblivion

INTRODUCTION:

Marla has a powerful and compelling need for daily exercise. She does any one of four options that may be available: outdoor biking, rollerblading, ice skating, or hiking uphill on <u>Mt. Royal</u>*. Weather permitting, vigorous biking is her first choice.

Because of the dullness and tedium, using an indoor bicycle or a treadmill is not acceptable to Marla. She also finds that walking outdoors on flat ground is boring and does not burn sufficient calories.

A daily exercise workout is not always possible. Since the Butler Building is without walls on two sides, with little protection from the elements, rollerblading is frequently not practical. The ice rink, available to Marla from late March through May, allows for only one session per week of daylight, recreational skating. Traveling to Mt. Royal necessitates car transportation which she may not have. Montreal's extreme weather rules out biking most days of the year and the three alternatives can be problematic.

Any day when none of the four options are feasible, in a distraught mood Marla puts herself into a state of *oblivion* - a potion of alcohol and pills to induce hours of deep sleep.

All her life, a power blackout has been one of her worst fears. During a lengthy outage and to escape the mental torture of inactivity, she retreats into oblivion.

Thinking of the future, Marla would seek the oblivion of extended sedation, if it should ever be necessary to avoid the stress of an illness, surgery or a medical condition resulting in food or exercise restrictions.

Text:
Daily exercise is an indispensable routine; I despise anything that interferes with it, as happens so often, during the misery of winter. When unable to bike, besides being deprived of exercise, it also prevents grocery shopping. (See Chapter 10 - Food Shopping)

When cheated of a daily exercise workout, (one of four options, mentioned in the Introduction) and not a single one available, my brain races with disappointment and anger. Since there is no acceptable substitute, my only alternative is an escape into the deep sleep of *oblivion*.

While I know that seeking oblivion with alcohol and drugs is not a healthy practice, it is a better substitute than day-long boredom and endless noshing. If I attempted to make it through the day without exercise and refrain from deep sleep, all I'd do is whine and complain to everyone around me. I might also telephone Father and others driving them nuts with my uncontrollable despair. (See Chapter 7 - Meltdowns)

Confined to the apartment, with no chance for exercise, I would suffer from cabin fever*, characterized by anxiety, restlessness, boredom and even regression. If not opting for oblivion, I might regress to childish behavior - angrily, tearing paper, and flinging it everywhere!

Being a state of total unawareness, I derive no pleasure from oblivion per se; yet this nothingness is preferable to an agony of discontent and food cravings.

When I awaken, the negative emotions can race back. There are times when the Valium pills and alcohol fail to keep me asleep the entire day and I wake up in mid-afternoon - hungry, restless, and miserable! I then seek a second dose of oblivion, go back to bed, and get more sleep.

A short attention span caused by my Attention Deficit Disorder prevents me from spending a day indoors - doing passive activities, such as reading or watching TV. If I don't exercise, there are physical symptoms of bloating and a feeling of bodily discomfort. (See Chapter 5)

Because of miserable weather, sometimes my only workout option is to rollerblade in the Butler Building. The bureaucrat who dreamed up a structural design - without south and east walls - must have been mentally deficient! Sometimes, after I do a short period of skating, the concrete floor gets drenched by a sudden downpour. With the floor slippery and dangerous, I admit defeat and return home - often crying the whole way!

On one such occasion, I was so agitated that I severely chewed and bloodied both arms. I then swallowed four Valium pills with a glass of booze and got into bed. This time the oblivion included a *dark mood*, not caring whether, or not, I ever woke up! (See Chapter 35 - Suicidal Thoughts)

Since winter exercise is often unavailable, I wish a scientist could arrange my hibernation, putting me in a dormant state until spring.

In recent winters, with virtually no exercise possible, there were days I would go on strike, refrain from going to work and remain in bed the whole day except for a few hours in the evening.

I notice opposite reactions to my oblivion. Some people express disapproval for the wasted time I spend conked-out and suggest constructive activities to substitute for a day's loss of exercise. In contrast, a few others will make sarcastic remarks that I am so lucky to enjoy a deep slumber in mid-day and wish they could do the same!

I could never abide by their so-called "constructive activities," like shopping at the mall, knitting a sweater, reading novels, and one even suggested volunteer work! Being deprived of exercise and staying awake, I can barely focus on anything but constant eating. They fail to understand that my best option, by far, is oblivion.

Living on my own, Mother began tolerating the oblivion; she would say: "Take your damn pills and go to bed!" That was her way of shutting me up, because on days without exercise she'd get disgusted with my phone calls of whining and bitching non-stop!

My father will occasionally express disapproval of my oblivion. Yet, at other times, when I'm fearfully complaining about some bad weather, ongoing or predicted, he sarcastically tells me to get "zonked." As was the case with Mother, he cannot tolerate the whining and grumbling.

Admittedly, doing oblivion is wasting my life, but is the only way I can avoid the cabin fever of staying housebound and plagued with intense food cravings. My drugged sleep of erased consciousness is nothing to brag about, but I cannot help but extol its virtues; it is my best and *only* way to overcome the bitter days of no exercise.

Others can enjoy an alternate activity when the "real thing" is not available; while for me, it simply won't wash.

CONCLUSION:
On a single day, when all four of Marla's exercise options are unavailable, she feels gloom and doom! The only alternative is oblivion since there is nothing else! The sugary saying, "This too shall pass," has never been her outlook; so that being without exercise is a setback that only her loss of consciousness can overcome.

In the next chapter, it is time to lambaste people and services that have disappointed Marla.

13

Four Letdowns

INTRODUCTION:
Throughout her adult life, Marla has been in desperate need of car rides and home care assistance. In 1997, Marla was introduced to Peter Zwack, president of the Autism Society of Montreal; in their conversations, he expressed a desire to help fulfill both needs. **(Letdown #1)**

<u>CLSC</u>* Montreal social services is a public agency with staff trained in psychotherapy. Their mission is to provide a multidisciplinary approach, adapted to the needs of clients requiring assistance. **(Letdown #2)**

Through the auspices of Canada Medicare, Marla is given a fifty-minute hour, per week, of psychiatric services. Her prime requirements in therapy are to vent stressors that plague her and obtain supportive counsel, as needed. **(Letdown #3)**

JFS <u>Jewish Family Services</u>* offers a variety of services for individuals in the Montreal Jewish community and the community at large. It is financed by donations and membership fees. Marla joined JFS expecting to obtain occasional car rides to <u>Mt. Royal</u>*. **(Letdown #4)**

Text and the Peter Zwack runaround:
Before his untimely death, in 2005, Peter Zwack was a board member of Miriam Home, a local organization which serves the needs of developmentally disabled individuals who have a below average IQ. He was also president of the Montreal Autism Society and a Professor of Meteorology at a local university.

Peter's interest in autism began with his son who had the disorder. By providing no more than monthly meetings, the Autism Society offered none of the supportive services needed to improve my life. Because of the late hour and difficult travel conditions, I declined Peter's invitation to attend the meetings.

Also, his members were mildly autistic and interested primarily in self-improvement. I had nothing in common with them. They would not understand my Co-morbid personality and the depth of my autism; a lifestyle of basic survival which was all I could muster. I've learned from past experience that HFA* people, who are less seriously afflicted, are often hostile toward a severely autistic person, like myself, and will flame* me for not accomplishing more with my life. (See Chapter 21)

When I first spoke to Peter on the phone, he asked for a detailed account of my neurological condition. I provided the information and in subsequent conversations he was desirous of helping me.

Since he was a new person in my life, I arranged that he be interviewed by my Psychiatrist. The interview took place and Dr, Freedman concluded that Peter was not interested in me per se, but cared about a new program he hoped to get funded by the Quebec government. It was to consist of client training in social skills, finding employment, and home care know-how. Based on Dr. Freedman's evaluation, Peter's plans were not in synch with my special needs; however, being desperate, I nevertheless kept in touch with Peter, hopeful the new program, if funded, would provide me with car rides and housekeeping assistance. (See Chapter 14)

As time progressed during the first three years of our acquaintance, he kept making vague promises to get me the tangible help I was seeking. Then, suddenly out of the blue, he asked for a list of my behavior problems and their triggers. I mistakenly thought he would use the information to address my special needs.

Turns out, Peter was of no help and proved to be a devious person. Without consulting me, he handed the list to my CLSC social worker and requested that she locate a Behavior Modification specialist to help me eradicate a number of my surface behaviors. There was no follow-up by my social worker for a treatment, she knew from our previous conversations, I would never agree to. (See Chapter 16)

Realizing that Peter's sole intent was to get me started on Behavior Modification, a treatment abhorrent to me, I cooled our relationship and for several months we hardly spoke. (See Chapter 16)

Due to Mother's tragic death, January 2000, it had me believe that Peter, because of my loss, might now try harder to get me supportive help. As a matter of fact, he acknowledged my rejection of behavior mod and agreed the only help of value, for me, would be <u>tangible support</u>*, namely car rides and kitchen help. He promised to contact an organization who would fund the services that CLSC and JFS could not deliver. Nothing came of his promise.

In 2003, a grant was approved by the Quebec government to finance a program that would aid HFA adults. Peter promised I'd be the very first client and he'd work with Miriam Home to fulfill my special needs. I waited in vain but nothing materialized.

I tried to contact Peter, who was frequently out of town; it took months before I could reach him. When I finally made contact, he suggested I speak with my social worker, who could obtain from Miriam Home precise information about the HFA program.

As it turned out, my social worker refused to contact Miriam Home until she first spoke with Peter, who was never available. She did, however, learn that the program had indeed begun but would make no effort to get information, as to the services being offered. I then contacted Miriam Home but they would not talk with me directly, referring me back to my social worker. As the victim of a runaround, I got nowhere with either of them.

My only hope was to contact Peter; but ignoring my e-mails and many phone messages, it became obvious that Peter had washed his hands of me.

CLSC (Montreal Social Services):

My autism, dyspraxia and other disabilities do not qualify for basic help that I need for survival in the mainstream. Government regulations would only allow for material aid if I was incapable of doing one, or more, of the following: feed myself, walk freely, use the toilet and bathe myself. (I still receive from CLSC an inadequate one hour of home care per week, begun several years ago and so far has not been rescinded.)

Despite my desperate cry for help, tangible assistance is not forthcoming! CLSC cannot provide it, and there is no CLSC social worker willing to do a search on my behalf; that is, locate a foundation or charity willing to provide funding for home care assistance and essential car rides. I have lost all hope.

Psychiatrist:

When Dr. Freedman, my psychiatrist of over 30 years, died in 2004, it was difficult to find a replacement. The only psychiatrist who had an opening was Dr. Webster (pseudonym).

Unlike Dr. Freedman, who was supportive, Dr. Webster's philosophy adheres to the principal that everyone has the ability to overcome their neurological disorders; it's purely a matter of determination and unrelenting effort.

He is opposed to my need for supportive counseling. Instead, he advocates "mind games" that smack of behavior modification, a type of treatment I could never withstand, due to my poor thought focusing ability; nor do I have the least interest in throwing away my true personality.

JFS (Jewish Family Services):
When biking is not possible, because of inclement weather, walking the trail on Mt. Royal is usually my only exercise option. Yet with JFS, I no longer qualify for their car service to the mountain; a new JFS policy, allows rides only for scheduled appointments, education classes, and job locations. (See Chapter 12 - Exercise or Oblivion)

CONCLUSION:
Peter Zwack, CLSC, Dr. Webster and JFS are not unique; they typify other letdowns occurring throughout Marla's life.

To lead any semblance of a satisfactory, independent life in the mainstream, all Marla needs is a modicum of human assistance, namely: occasional car rides, supportive psychotherapy, verbal support, and home care. With those essential helps, she'd be able to continue holding down a job and lead a more desirable life; otherwise, her future looks bleak. (See Chapter 35 - Situational Depression - Suicidal Thoughts)

In Chapter 14, Marla discusses Dr. Freedman, her late psychiatrist for over three decades.

14

Psychiatrist and Medications

INTRODUCTION:
In January, 2004, Dr. Hyman Freedman, psychiatrist, suffered an onset of cancer, terminating Marla's three decades of counseling sessions with him.

Beginning at age 14, seeing him on a weekly basis, it was an opportunity to vent emotions, discuss interpersonal problems, receive supportive counsel, gain new perspectives, and learn more about autism.

Both father and mother were in favor of their daughter receiving psychotherapy. They viewed her quirky behaviors as treatable emotional problems and, by receiving treatment, she would begin to function normally.

Text:
Dr. Freedman was well-aware of my acute Autism. He acknowledged my dislike of social activities, lack of interest in stylish clothes, my deep-seated inflexibility, and ongoing people problems. (See Chapter 2)

As my therapist, he was sympathetic when my parents forced me into stressful social activities. He accepted my preference for being a loner and was aware that I lacked motivation to acquire social skills.

I recall his sessions with my parents, providing insight into my autism, or as he called it, <u>Asperger syndrome</u>*. (Believing that the word "autism" would have negative connotations, he therefore opted for the "milder" Asperger label - a type of high functioning autism.)

There were numerous supportive deeds done on my behalf. Dr. Freedman suggested to my parents they no longer interfere with my disinterest in wearing trendy clothes.

He was successful in convincing them to accept my dislike of social functions - recommending that I attend few in number, perhaps an occasional wedding, bar mitzvah, or funeral. At home, to keep the peace, I mostly went along with this compromise.

In their disapproval of my doing uncontrollable Tourette tics, he believed their hollering, threats and mimicry were totally inappropriate. (See Chapter 6)

During the teen years, I was having even greater trouble coping with life at home, and he was most supportive.

In 1995, when <u>CLSC</u>* social services planned to discontinue my one hour per week of home care assistance, he wrote a compelling letter to the agency that had it continued.

Feeling that the position of Medical Library Assistant was essential to my psychological and financial well- being, he offered to explain my neurological condition and special needs to any new head librarian, becoming my supervisor. Also, if I should ever be threatened with dismissal, he would surely intervene, on my behalf, with the nursing home administration. (See Chapter 26)

When the disability income tax credit was introduced in the mid-1980's, he filled out the necessary paperwork; and by justifying my special needs, I was granted the tax break

In 2001, the federal tax department sent me a letter planning to discontinue my tax credit. Enclosed was a detailed questionnaire that Dr. Freedman filled out and submitted. Subsequently, he received a second questionnaire, requiring more information about my impaired mental functioning; needless to say, he also complied with that request.

Still not satisfied, a government representative telephoned him and took a full hour asking additional questions about my disability. Dr. Freedman emphasized my enormous effort in continuing to work, even on a part-time basis. He said I could hardly support myself and despite a low income, I had never sought public assistance, always paid my taxes, and due to mental impairment, I was surely entitled to continued tax relief. Thanks to his efforts, in September 2002, I received a notice of continuance with the stipulation of having to justify the renewal every five years.

In our counseling sessions, one of the traits that made him so very special was his ability to compartmentalize. He was able to put aside all extraneous matters and with understanding and compassion, gave focused attention to whatever issues were troubling me. For example, he had to cancel a session, in 1990, when his son was badly hurt in a car accident. But he then returned the following week - caring and supportive as ever - even though his son was still far from recovering; Dr. Freedman's focus on my treatment never faltered.

However, there was occasionally an inconsistency in his spoken words. Sometimes, he was critical of my upbringing, yet at other times he considered my parents' disciplinary methods essentially *normal*, the way most <u>HFA</u>* youngsters were raised.

In 1997, I noticed that Dr. Freedman was losing his trait of being patient with me; it was at a time he mentioned his plans for semi-retirement. Frankly, I *exploded* and experienced sheer terror that he would be less available for our weekly sessions. He must have been annoyed at what was, apparently, my self-serving reaction.

In the final years of our doctor-client relationship, I noticed sullen moods at the very start of each weekly session. I suspected something was amiss in his life that lessened his usual caring and support. Unbeknownst to me at the time, he had been suffering from gastro-esophageal reflux disease.

His therapy continued dealing with my problems in getting along with co-workers and my other difficulties in the workplace. But, at the same time, he became less caring about personal issues bugging me: problems obtaining affordable low calorie Food, hardships in preparing meals, lack of daily Exercise and getting only crumbs of support from people I knew. He told me that unless I was able to pay for services rendered, it was unrealistic to expect <u>psychological</u>* and/or <u>tangible support</u>* from anyone. (See Chapters 10 and 12, respectively.)

I told him that with my scrimpy part-time income, I could ill afford to pay individuals for their kindness; my only hope was in finding one or two Good Samaritans, willing to be supportive and not expect payment.

Dr. Freedman was one of the few therapists who did not force change on patients. He acknowledged that my autistic inflexibility was hardwired and never pushed me toward becoming a *false* person in conflict with my true essence. However, he made it clear there was a heavy price to pay. He predicted a life of turmoil and suffering for being at odds with society and not adapting to the environment around me. As for my hatred of Montreal plus a dislike of Canada, he wanted me to face reality; the fact that a change of permanent locale - away from Canada - was not possible due to my limited financial circumstances. (See Chapter 9)

In the struggle with household chores, high food prices, and lack of exercise Dr. Freedman predicted my discontent would continue. He blamed it on my autistic Inflexibility, a refusal to compromise and settle for whatever life had to offer. (See Chapter 29)

The ability to do self-care, walk by myself, and eat without assistance was Dr. Freedman's standard for managing on my own. Since I could also work part-time, he thought I was exceptionally capable and not in need of financial aid or support from family members, co-workers, acquaintances, social services, or anyone else.

I disagreed with his criteria of what constitutes "managing;" it requires lots more than toileting, walking, and eating. My personal life was still in a shambles; he failed to consider my anti-social behavior, Self-Abuse, and Suicidal Thoughts. (See Chapters 11 and 35, respectively.)

Since he knew about my need for frequent Oblivion, his concept of "managing" should have conflicted with knowing how often I sit in the house, suffering from lack of exercise. And to prevent hours of boredom, I go into a deep sleep, made possible by sleeping pills and gulps of cheap wine! (See Chapter 12)

While some of the parental meetings with Dr. Freedman had been helpful, pertaining to clothes and social issues, I later feared bringing Father and Dr. Freedman together for any additional discussions. My father would have expressed his wish to take extended vacations and my therapist would have encouraged it, by saying: "Marla must learn to manage her life and not rely on you for support." If he followed such advice and being my only support for car rides and other help, my life would be kaput - a recipe for <u>cabin fever</u>*, despair and oblivion. (See Chapter 4)

A preponderance of mental health professionals are of the opinion that once offspring vacate the family nest, parents are no longer responsible for the well-being of adult children. Included in this generalization would be someone like me. Though not *legally* obligated, I believe there is a moral responsibility for parents to provide, as best they can, tangible and psychological support based on their adult offspring's situational needs.

I once suggested that Dr. Freedman discuss with my father the need for arranging backup support, with a friend or relative, whenever he planned to be out of town. My therapist responded in a way that infuriated me; he said it was unrealistic to expect my father or anyone else to provide supportive services, unless I had a physical handicap such as hand amputation or paralysis!

I vehemently disagreed. While my "neurological baggage" is not apparent to the naked eye, I am in fact suffering from several extreme disabilities that I believe should qualify me for supportive intervention. (See Chapter 21 - Co-morbid and Invisible)

For example, I require daily psychological support - an evening phone call - to discuss the day's happenings and vent any difficulties that transpired. Also, occasional tangible support is needed for food shopping and/or a car ride to Mt. Royal. (See Chapter 12 - Exercise)

Dr. Freedman knew that bad weather did not permit biking, but for mildly inclement weather, I had the exercise option of climbing Mt. Royal. However, for transportation to and from the mountain, I needed tangible support. With no empathy for my financial plight, I could not believe my ears when he suggested I take round-trip taxicab rides, and not depend on my father or anyone else. His suggestion was ludicrous, since cabs are costly and by working part-time, I was subsisting at the poverty level!

Nor did my psychiatrist feel empathy for my housekeeping problems. As with some men, he did not consider home care a priority and told me I should do no more cleaning than was absolutely necessary; all that really mattered was that the apartment not attract bugs or make me ill. (See Chapter 11 - Chores)

Dr. Freedman had always assumed that CLSC (social services) would never give me any home care services and was surprised when Tammy - a volunteer community worker - convinced CLSC to provide me with light housekeeping assistance, and it was approved for a single hour, one day a week! If Tammy, with so little clout, was able to get me a paltry one hour, I wonder how many additional hours Dr. Freedman, a reputable psychiatrist, could have prevailed on CLSC; much to my disappointment, he made no such attempt.

As for my problems in doing kitchen chores, all my therapist could suggest was hiring a housekeeper! It should have been obvious; I could not afford hired help. And the only other options were restaurants I could ill afford, or frozen TV dinners of mostly junk food cooked in the microwave, and certainly not the healthful food I depend on.

Eventually, my parents helped me finance a decent condo but made me agree not to smash up the kitchen. To placate them, my felt rage is now discharged in biting my arms. Dr. Freedman made another proposal that was even more unrealistic than his costly taxicab rides solution. In noticing the welts and scabs, he suggested that I not bite my arms but resume my destructive behavior. He knew that in previous apartments, I uncontrollably demolished the kitchen and was held responsible for hundreds of dollars in repairs. I found it hard to believe he would suggest defying my parents, by returning to a ruinous practice that we could ill-afford.

Speaking of his limitations, when I was no longer in academia, he was primarily interested in discussing issues that negatively affected my job. Actually, most of the problems that bugged me were outside of work and occurred later in the day. Somehow he did not consider personal issues particularly relevant to my treatment. I disagreed.

In addition to job difficulties, he should have given his attention to my other problems, such as: affordable food, the wretched environment, loathsome weather, and many issues of the Quickening. (See Chapter 34)

Despite having had decades of psychotherapy with Dr. Freedman, my life had become increasingly difficult. Negative moods, driven by <u>situational depression,</u>* had worsened. The experience was a more significant brain disconnect between rational thinking and emotional acting-out behavior.

All he could offer were antidepressants which I consistently refused. In fact, I had recently given him an essay by Dr. Amitta <u>Shah</u>*, supporting my unwillingness to take antidepressants. It states that HFA people are especially prone to some of the drug side effects, including bizarre acting-out behavior and even suicide.

Dr. Freedman believed that my bad moods and emotional suffering were caused by a mental state that he labeled "a decreased ability to sense happiness," an abnormal mind process that he thought could be alleviated with medications.

Convinced that I lacked the *neurological equipment* to cope with the knocks of daily living, from time-to-time, Dr. Freedman made suggestions that I try various psychiatric drugs; then after reading some literature about each one, the decision was always mine, whether or not, to give one of them a try. As each med failed in various ways, mostly due to intolerable side effects, he often felt I should have continued a medication somewhat longer - allowing my nervous system to get accustomed to it.

Trazodone cut down some of my kitchen rage behavior, but only for a few months. I was miserable as ever that harsh winter, deprived of exercise. As a side effect, the med had me wakeup, every night with blocked nostrils, requiring nose drops. Since the drug was proving worthless, I gave it up.

I also tried Luvox, an <u>SSRI</u>* similar to Prozac. It did nothing but give me nausea and fragmented sleep. Since the nausea never abated, after six months, I quit taking the drug.

Next was Tofranil, which <u>Temple Grandin</u>* said eased her Anxiety and Sensory Integration Disorder. She claimed that low doses of the antidepressant helps autistics with those symptoms. Apparently, Tofranil does not work for everyone, since the drug did nothing but increase my appetite. (See Chapters 7 and 18, respectively.)

Another drug I tried was Risperdal which was an antipsychotic (not an antidepressant). With sluggish side effects, it made me unmotivated to do anything but eat. It dulled my mind so much, I was incapable of writing an e-mail until the day's drug effects wore off. It put me into a limbo state, lethargic to do anything worthwhile, yet so restless that when I tried dozing, it was impossible to fall asleep.

Buspar, an anti-anxiety drug, was also a fiasco. Like an antidepressant or antipsychotic, it works by gradually modifying brain chemistry during continued use. But for me the side effect was immediate and severe; I suffered migraines every two days and could not sleep.

It became apparent to me that instead of dangerous drugs, what I needed was a change of locale; the harsh environment was my over-whelming problem. Montreal's atrocious climate is responsible for much of my situational depression and irritability, cruel weather systems keep me housebound most of the year. (See Chapter 9 - Montreal and Climate)

During our later years together, Dr. Freedman was disappointed in my refusal to try any further medications. Seeing no improvement in my behavior and moods, he said it was my decision whether or not to take an antidepressant; but it came with his dire warning: "If you refuse to take a drug because of mild side effects, you will pay a steep price with greater unhappiness."

Dr. Freedman thought I'd eventually find a med that would help improve my living situation. Turns out, he was totally mistaken; nothing on this earth could trick my brain into tolerating a city that, for me, is all wrong and in conflict with my daily <u>routines</u>*; without them, life is not worth living!

Dr. Freedman never understood my discontent with Montreal. He enjoyed living there, claiming the city offered everything a person could desire. I did not expect him to necessarily agree with my opposing point of view, but wished he had sufficient empathy to realize, that based on my needs, the city is terribly inadequate. Believing that my negative personality was the problem, he would exclaim, "Marla, you'd be unhappy no matter where you live!"

For me, his opinion of Montreal was irrelevant because as a man of means, his affluent lifestyle was totally different from mine. Also, since I've never lived anywhere else, he was wrong in asserting I'd be unhappy wherever I resided. As my supportive therapist, he needed to envision my point of view, plus a willingness to validate whatever made sense, from *my* perspective.

As for my Passive Aggressive behavior, Dr. Freedman was not critical and considered my need to "settle the score" as petty from a monetary standpoint; a routine that consisted mainly of damaging inexpensive junk Food, in supermarkets. He was also aware that no amount of his scolding would compel me to quit a vandalism behavior that gave me so much satisfaction! (See Chapters 33 and 10, respectively)

Dr. Freedman in drawing a parallel with other HFA adults, who had improved their lives, he thought it was time I began making a better life adjustment. He failed to take into account the scope and depth of my multiple disorders. These, in addition to HFA, were making my condition far more debilitating, compared to others afflicted with fewer disorders and less co-morbidity.

Dr. Freedman once asked me why I considered Dyspraxia and Sensory Integration Disorder more debilitating than autism. I told him that because of dyspraxia, my poor hand-eye coordination troubles me throughout the day. As for sensory integration disorder, my life would be less stressful if textures did not bug me, and the hated kitchen sounds did not cause me to become a growling beast. I can get by with my autism and not have a social life, whereas blundering hands and Kitchen Chores are daily crises, unless one can afford hired help! (See Chapters 17, 18 and 11, respectively.)

Although, I had what Dr. Freedman considered were several secondary conditions, he believed autism was the central disorder, affecting me most acutely and causing most of life's difficulties - especially social impairments and lack of flexibility.

With autism, his forte, and being less familiar with my other disorders, he chose not to seriously deal with them. Actually, autism is just one facet of my dysfunctional brain; what makes my condition difficult to improve is the complexity of multiple dysfunctions, and not just autism. My other afflictions should have been considered by him and also treated in their own right.

People with multiple disorders find it difficult to locate a mental health professional with an ability to comprehend, even in a general way, the full extent of their miserable life.

As in my case, a dysfunctional brain can be complex, involving multiple disorders, with Co-morbid features and traits acting in synergy*, so that psychotherapy should be viewed as an unfolding, learning process, for both client and professional. (See Chapter 21)

On the topic of exercise, Dr. Freedman could not understand why I was unable to tolerate a single day without it. He said I needed to face the reality of occasional inclement weather, so that a daily bike ride is not always feasible. I considered his remark, a blind spot in his thinking; an inability to comprehend and validate what I believed was a legitimate mind-set.

Dr. Freedman would assert that born with autism, I would have turned out the same way, regardless of my upbringing. I'm surprised it was not obvious to him that a childhood of verbal abuse and rejection had to worsen my personality and in all liklihood, the damage would prevail the rest of my life.

He didn't expect me to make progress socially, but considering my good ability in holding down a responsible job, he thought of me as a relatively successful HFA person. What he found disappointing was my unhappiness, inflexibility and dysfunctional behavior patterns that after years of therapy, I had not become a more, well-adjusted person.

In summary, I can disagree with several of Dr. Freedman's viewpoints, yet overall he was supportive and caring. I am grateful that he fully understood the severity of my autism, and did not pressure me with acquiring a sociable demeanor. I could never have survived life, in the mainstream, had it not been for his weekly counsel.

Dr. Freedman was uniquely kind to accept me on a supportive treatment basis and as it turns out, there is no replacement. I live in a society of mental health professionals who only counsel patients who are willing to accept methodology, such as OT*, behavior modification and other forms of short-term treatment - designed to make changes in a client's thinking and behavior; for such programs I would find little or no value; since my poor life adjustment is fundamentally situational, forced to live in a wretched environment, without sufficient money to relocate. (See Chapter 16 - Behavior Modification and Chapter 9 - Montreal and Climate)

ADDENDUM:
Dr. Hyman Freedman died on June 9, 2004.

The following tribute written by Marla Comm was read by the officiating rabbi during funeral services on June 11th.

EULOGY:
I was born with high functioning autism and for almost 33 years was seen by Dr. Freedman for supportive psychotherapy. I knew him for so long and shared so much of my life with him that he felt like a part of my family. I told him things I never told anyone else. He helped me through my turbulent teen years, as well as the trials and tribulations of life as a disabled adult in hard times. He was the only person who accepted me as I was and did not judge me. His office was a haven, the only place where I felt safe and protected.

More than just a therapist, he was my pillar of strength. He was a fighter who didn't give in to anything. Nothing held him back. In all the years I knew him, I had only two unexpected cancellations. He even kept his appointments during the 1998 ice storm and July 1987 flood. He adhered so faithfully to his scheduled appointments that they became the framework that held my life together. The exceptional health he enjoyed until this tragic illness struck him, infused me with hope and reminded me that it was possible to stay active and healthy in midlife and old age.

He also went beyond the call of duty as my therapist and let me call him at home during crises. Out of the goodness of his heart he continued seeing me after I reached adulthood. During the winter he drove me home after sessions.

His passing left a huge hole in my life that nothing will ever replace. I miss him badly.

15

Interpersonal Validation

INTRODUCTION:
Interpersonal validation occurs when someone confirms what we say. For Marla, the need for validation is critically needed and unrelenting. With Dr. Freedman, her psychiatrist of many years, she looked to him for his verbal support. Since his death, whatever validation she now receives comes from her father, co-workers, acquaintances, and pen pals. (See Chapter 14)

Now an adult, it is believed that much of her validation is sought to compensate for a verbally abusive childhood, during which time Marla's very essence and atypical thought patterns were repudiated by both parents. Her adult requirement for interpersonal validation is partly the result of low self-confidence.

Text:
My Borderline Personality traits create a need for interpersonal validation. (See Chapter 32) Dr. Freedman also believed that I needed the certainty of supportive validation, due to having an intermittent anxiety-stress disorder. (See Chapter 7 - Anxiety)

I need others to validate my insistence that the new millennium has brought hard times in a changed world. By suggesting additional perspectives, Dr. Freedman attempted to validate - in more realistic terms - my gnawing sensibilities and helped me find better ways to mentally cope with the ongoing global chaos. (See Chapter 34 - The Quickening)

There are co-workers and others who take delight in harassing me. When I've been the victim of teasing or verbal abuse, as a way of feeling better, I relate the incident to a few obliging people, seeking validation, and their agreeing I've been wronged.

Life in Montreal encompasses an atrocious climate, poor food availability and abrasive people. Outdoor exercise and human civility are often denied me. I need others to validate these <u>stressors</u>*; so when someone listens and responds, in a caring way, the misery is temporarily softened.

When discussing with an acquaintance the need for car rides to <u>Mt. Royal</u>* or for grocery shopping, it is not so much a desire for validation, rather the remote possibility this very person might provide some of the transportation, I must have.

I am angered when others do not verbally acknowledge these deficits in my life - a necessary first step in getting tangible help. These people expect me to be independent and not depend on others for support. At times, despite my best efforts at explanation, my needs are not verbally validated; then in spoken frustration, I rebound with flaming anger!

I count on others to at least acknowledge that for me, Montreal is the wrong place to live. Admittedly, interpersonal validation conversations rarely provide any *material* help nor does anyone I know have the commitment or financial resources to get me out of this dung heap; yet, when I hear their kind words of agreement, it does lift my spirits.

In contrast, Dr. Freedman was reluctant to validate what I suffer in Montreal and instead he would extol the city's virtues. In his stock argument, he never mentioned the brutal snow, ice, strong winds, thunder storms and freezing rain that kept me housebound most of the year. Instead, he would praise what he called my good fortune to live in this great cosmopolitan city. It would then be followed by his viewpoint that Montreal was not the crux of my problem, because I had a fundamentally negative personality and would be unhappy anywhere! (See Chapter 9 – Montreal)

When <u>neurotypical</u>* individuals refuse to validate my dissatisfaction with Montreal, they usually offer banal advice:
**If certain food prices are high, you should find substitutes;
**if kitchen chores are a problem, use microwaveable TV dinners;
**if biking is impossible, take a brisk walk inside the mall;
**if someone utters a hostile remark, ignore it and walk away.

Sorry to disappoint them, but my hardwired inflexibility does not allow for alternate responses, except under rare circumstances.

Not only do some people not understand the inflexible nature of my reactions to life's problems, but they are often preoccupied with their own dilemmas and in no mood to deal with mine. Apropos, I have no interest in other people's difficulties and certainly no wish to help solve them.

Before people wake up and take my environmental plight seriously, maybe I need to get their full attention. Perhaps if I commit a crime, get arrested and thrown into prison, they will begin to realize that my case is more serious than previously thought. Maybe they will then, unequivocally, validate that Montreal has become my ruination! (See Chapter 35 - Suicidal Thoughts)

CONCLUSION:

Marla has an intense need to discuss with others her special needs plus life's many problems. She seeks interpersonal validation to confirm various truths based on her own reality.

Those who pay attention to Marla's problems will sometimes mention substitute solutions. These are rejected, out of hand! Severe autism has left Marla with virtually no flexibility, throughout most aspects of her lifestyle.

The next chapter discusses a psychiatric "mind game" treatment that Marla finds repulsive.

16

Behavior Modification

INTRODUCTION:
BMT behavior modification therapy is a form of psychotherapy that uses basic learning techniques to inhibit maladaptive behavior patterns. To be more in keeping with societal standards, it does this by teaching the client to substitute acceptable behaviors for undesirable ones.

An offshoot is CBT cognitive behavior therapy. It goes one step further by attempting to change, in essence, the *underlying, dysfunctional thought pattern* that is responsible for a client's unacceptable behavior.

Text:
I often display behaviors that society considers offensive such as verbal hostility, petty vandalism, self-mutilation and emotional melt-downs. Co-workers and acquaintances have suggested *self-discipline* as a means of discontinuing undesirable behaviors. In response to their advice, I reject anything that smacks of BMT or CBT.

Until I live in a city where my essential needs are being met, there can be no *modification* of what society considers my unacceptable, antisocial behavior. My basic requirements for a good life are daily exercise, healthful food, a hot dry climate, and home care assistance.

I once experimented with BMT. It all had to do with me smashing up the kitchen in junk apartments, as a way of venting anger, and then having to repair the costly damage. After living in several of them, my parents helped me buy a decent condo, with the proviso I not wreck anything. Therefore, as a substitute release of anger, instead of attacking the kitchen, I began to viciously bite my arms. (See Chapter 11 - Kitchen Chores and Self-Abuse)

Because self-mutilation on a conspicuous part of the body was a terrible alternative, I hit upon a ploy that would neither damage my arms nor wreck the kitchen. Using the principle of BMT, I put an inexpensive, replaceable worktable in the kitchen. The next time there was a need to vent anger; I began smashing the substitute table. To my surprise and disappointment, I felt no satisfaction; it did not give vent to my rage! The BMT experiment was a flop and the pent-up anger, worse than ever! With the promise made to my parents, the only remaining option was a continuation of self-abuse.

People suggest that a person with good intelligence can *learn* to do whatever it takes to behave normally. The word "learn" connotes behavior mod, which to me is a no-no.

The purpose of behavior mod is to substitute a more acceptable behavior for an undesirable one. For example, my social worker suggested that by writing life's complaints on a piece of paper and then tearing it up, it could take the place of venting my troubles to anyone who would listen which, by the way, is one of my annoying habits. The social worker's suggested tactic would surely meet with failure, because as I learned from the kitchen table experiment, my brain will not accept a substitute behavior for the *real thing*. It would also be rejected because unless someone was going to read the paper and verbally respond to it, my distraught emotions would get no relief.

I'm often given advice to change my bad attitudes and negative think-ing by using techniques of cognitive behavior therapy. Correcting a *thought pattern* is even more unyielding than changing one's out-ward behavior with BMT. Therefore, I consider CBT worthless and using it would surely result in failure.

People interpret, as laziness, my refusal to go through the rigors of BMT. Trying to convince them, otherwise, falls on deaf ears. They believe I should learn to restrain my own anger and try to better understand the reasons for someone's negative remarks. In truth, I have no wish to control my reactions and don't care one whit about anyone's disapproval. If provoked by someone, I will <u>flame</u>* them with an even greater amount of verbal poison; it is the payback that a numbskull deserves for starting up with me!

When already in a low mood, it is even more difficult to ignore the snide remarks made by others. CBT teaches the client to hide or suppress hurt feelings, while learning to better tolerate stressful situations. My response is simple: "I want no part of a therapy that rejects my personality." Now, in my late forties, it is impossible to change a lifelong behavior and compromise my true essence.

Early on, professional intervention could have made a difference in my life. At a youthful age, my dysfunctional behaviors were perhaps less rigid and somewhat amenable to change. In contrast, as a middle aged adult, the re-learning process would create inordinate stress. My hardwired, inappropriate behaviors - that give me satisfaction - have been mentally reinforced for decades. In addition, my Autism and its trait of inflexibility would resist any kind of personality "makeover." (See Chapter 2)

The only practical way to rid society of my dysfunctional behavior is by removing the triggers causing it; that is by a <u>Good Samaritan</u>* relocating me - far away - to a kinder, gentler and more appropriate environment.

CONCLUSION:

As an adult living in an abrasive city, with basic needs unmet and her CNS central nervous system in virtual burnout, Marla would be unable to withstand the rigors of behavior modification treatment, or anything similar.

If Marla's outward coping behavior were suppressed, it would leave her distraught. Since her neurological disorders are often triggers of "getting even," they bring forth emotions that provide Marla with considerable satisfaction.

Note:

Marla's Executive Function Disorder further decreases the likelihood that cognitive behavior therapy would be effective. An article in the *Journal of Geriatric Psychiatry and Neurology, 2005, June v.18, #2,* suggests that older adults with deficits in executive function skills often respond poorly to CBT. Although the article targets older people, it may also have relevance for Marla, approaching age 50. (See Chapter 20)

The next chapter explains why poor hand-eye coordination is perhaps Marla's most troublesome neurological disorder.

17

Dyspraxia

INTRODUCTION:
Marla suffers from dyspraxia and the most troubling symptom is her poor hand-eye coordination. She has difficulty doing fine-motor activities such as pouring liquids, writing, drawing, buttoning, and grasping objects.

For hand-eye coordination to properly function, the *brain* must use information received from Marla's vision to accurately determine where her hands and objects are positioned in space, and then be able to perform accurate hand movements. With dyspraxia, Marla is severely lacking in this skill, caused by a neural dysfunction of the brain and *not* a defect in her hands.

To a lesser degree, dyspraxia negatively affects her gross motor activities; the use of leg muscles for walking, running, skipping, dancing and jumping; all of which require strength, balance and coordination.

Text:
Although dyspraxia is a neurological disorder and recognized by a number of professionals in the United Kingdom, New Zealand and

a few other countries, it gets little credence in Canada or the US. Members of my Internet dyspraxia list goup* live mostly in the UK.

Nor has dyspraxia ever been listed in the index of the Diagnostic and Statistical Manual of Mental Disorders.

Even in the UK, recognition is sporadic. When seeking professional help, list group members complain that neurologists will refuse to attend an adult seeking a dyspraxia diagnosis. If the individual claims to be in need of treatment, physicians will insist that only children, not adults, have the condition.

In Canada, neurologists refer to poor dexterity as a "childhood developmental, coordination disorder," or "clumsy child syndrome," that a youngster gradually outgrows. Throughout my life, there has been no such improvement. As an adult, my poor hand-eye coordination is ongoing and getting progressively worse, as does other dyspraxic traits. (Unless the dysfunction is caused by trauma, it receives no medical recognition in Canada.)

For a youngster with dyspraxic symptoms, the purpose of providing early occupational therapy OT* or physiotherapy, is to enable better functioning of the arms, hands, feet and legs. To be successful, the treatment is best done at a young age when there is brain plasticity. The only "treatment" I received when knocking things over and causing spills was hollering, tongue-lashings, and told: "Stop being so damn clumsy!"

Stuck my entire life with the miseries of dyspraxia, more than anything else, I've wanted better functioning fine motor and gross motor skills. If playing a game required jumping, running or catching a ball, it was no fun being the neighborhood klutz.

In the workplace and at home - despite my best efforts to organize the clutter - I am rarely successful. This deficit is symptomatic of dyspraxia and is Co-morbid with my Executive Function Disorder. (See Chapter 21 and 20, respectively.)

The New Zealand Dyspraxia Association has a <u>website</u>* on the Internet. One article states that during a child's formative years, if early professional intervention is provided, children with dyspraxia, in many cases, will grow up to have rewarding, productive lives. In contrast, those not receiving intervention typically become unhappy, frustrated adults; many are unable to work and generally have dysfunctional lives. Despite lifelong suffering from extreme dyspraxia, I never received any treatment, and except for having a part time job, fraught with problems, the New Zealand description of a loser, parallels my life.

My sense of balance, which is a gross motor skill, has actually improved over the years from learning to do basic ice skating, rollerblading and biking. In contrast, the fine motor skills have continued to worsen with my hands not the problem; they would actually work properly if certain nerves and muscles were reliably connected to functioning neurons in the brain.

During Childhood and throughout my life, I have resisted all human contact. However, it is well known and essential that a baby receive physical stimulation for proper neurological development. Parental touching, cuddling and hugging would have benefited my nervous system and may have served to lessen the severity of what later became extreme dyspraxic malfunction.

In raising me, Mother never had the maternal instinct to insist on small amounts of physical contact, based on what little I could begin to tolerate; so that perhaps in time, I'd get used to more-and-more closeness. Unfortunately, both parents accepted my aloofness, so that my nervous system never received the hands-on stimulation that is required for normal development. (See Chapters 1 and 3, respectively.)

Knowing that my personality had always been rebellious, stubborn and negative, my Psychiatrist exclaimed: "As an infant, despite any parental effort, you would have rejected physical contact and not permitted any kind of hands-on therapy." He may well have been wrong and I fault my parents for never having sought appropriate, professional counsel. (See Chapter 14)

My hands were clumsy but had no influence on what Mother made me wear. For example, the clothes she bought never had pockets for items like Kleenex and sticks of gum; what I had to wear was always impractical, requiring fumbling adjustments, outfitted with buttons and bows, and made awkward because of poor dexterity.

I was never taken to a neurologist to evaluate my precarious hand - eye coordination and other klutzy problems. My parents believed the bumbling and awkwardness could be overcome through lots of practice and sheer effort - it was *all* up to me!

In kindergarten, I was the last kid in the class to master skills like tying my shoelaces and buttoning my coat; with much fumbling, I was the slowest one to get ready.

As for creative art ability, I recall a teacher telling me that my picture resembled a mud pie. Throughout grade school, I was frustrated when I had to do a drawing because I could never get pictures to come out the way I visualized them. Getting my brain to control my hand movements bordered on the impossible. Since ripping-up the art paper and starting over was the usual outcome, I never finished a single drawing!

Written assignments in school or at home were always messy. Early on, I tried to learn touch-typing but failed because of poor dexterity and an inability to memorize the keyboard layout. (See Chapter 8 - Attention Deficit Disorder) Typing was stressful due to erratic movements of my fingers easily pressing the wrong keys.

Eventually, by having a valued computer, typing a letter became a lot easier and mistakes easily corrected. And by using the "hunt and peck system," I was able to produce an error-free, final output.

Doing chores in the kitchen is a much different story. I am forever spilling things. The simple act of yanking off the tab on a soda can easily creates a mess of sticky liquid splattered all over the place! (See Chapter 11 - Kitchen Chores)

To solve the soft drink problem, people have suggested buying my soda in two-liter plastic bottles. Turns out, all it did was create a new set of problems. The bottle is awkward and slips from my grasp when holding it in one hand and trying to turn the cap with my other hand; it invariably leads to a spill. I have trouble accurately pouring the soda into a glass, causing more spillage. As for the soda can, I have the advantage of drinking directly from it. There is no panacea; bottles and cans all give me trouble, each in their own way.

Because of kitchen problems, my psychiatrist recommended that I hire a housekeeper or simply refrain from preparing meals at home. I thought he knew that with my skimpy income of part-time employment, I could neither afford hired help nor the cost of restaurant food.

Others have recommended I subsist on microwave TV dinners. These are pricey and unhealthy - full of starch, fat, salt and sugar - leading to obesity and sickness. I easily shot down what I considered a stupid suggestion!

Besides the torture of preparing a meal, countless other *ordinary* tasks give me trouble: fiddling with the key in a lock, unwrapping a package, holding a cup of liquid, grasping an object, opening a three-ring notebook, and so on.

In addition, there are mundane tasks in the workplace that cause frustration and deplete my energy. These include punching the number codes on magnetic locks, striking a time-clock, and by entering passwords in the computer, gaining access to the many databases we use.

As for personal care, even though there is little visual function when brushing my teeth, proper hand movement is important. I'm supposed to reach all areas of the mouth and apply the right pressure while brushing. Dental hygienists have been telling me for years that the pressure I apply is uneven; they can detect inadequate brushing because a number of teeth have more plaque than others; while some are excessively worn from being brushed too hard.

Due to poor hand-eye coordination, getting dressed and undressed presents problems. This is yet another reason to justify my relocation to a warm, dry climate so as to free myself from wearing layers of winter clothes - a dyspraxic burden that involves boots, coats, sweaters, scarves and other paraphernalia.

Whenever I go biking, due to a city ordinance, I have to fiddle with putting on a bothersome safety helmet; and on hot summer days I suffer the additional discomfort of perspiration running down my face and neck.

My poor sense of spatial awareness is yet another dyspraxia symptom. In small areas, I have a slow response time among individuals moving in random and unpredictable directions. I also lack ability to judge distances. Although my eyes can see what's around me, my brain fails to correctly process the linear information. As a result, I bump into people, especially in a supermarket or a busy section of the mall. I always avoid skating among wild kids because with my slow reaction time, a head-on collision is an accident waiting to happen!

In Montreal, biking is hazardous. Motorists drive their cars with abandon as if the city streets are racetracks! When cycling, my reaction time is quite good. Not having that ability, I could easily get knocked down by a speeding car or a driver changing lanes and not signaling.

A poor sense of direction is another trait common to dyspraxics. When biking, I can easily lose my way, especially in areas where the streets are curved and irregular. I also have trouble finding my way in complicated buildings, such as the university library. The entire structure is oddly shaped with curved hallways that have me confused, not unlike the irregular streets.

Although dyspraxic <u>fine motor</u>* problems are the most debilitating, my <u>gross motor</u>* skills have also been problematic. I could not participate in ball games or do gym activities in school. I was awkward at dancing, did not have proper swimming technique, and it required three years of painstaking effort, learning how to ride a bike.

On the ice rink, the instructor remarked that I was much slower at learning how to skate than most other adults. The best I could do was learn basic skating movements, devoid of style and grace. Learning to rollerblade was a similar experience, but somewhat easier.

I have noticed that any stress in the environment worsens my dyspraxia. When I am overloaded with too much worry and nervous tension, the circuits connecting my brain with hand muscles tend to shut down. All it takes is a morning of nerve-racking grocery shopping to leave me with hands that are barely able to move - unable to put the groceries away or even begin preparing a meal.

As with all my other disorders, I have trouble getting people to understand my dyspraxic coordination problems. In fact, I am still struggling to educate my father. Although this neurological dysfunction has been ongoing all my life - over forty years - he is still in denial. To this day, he still wonders why I spill things and cause all kinds of messes when working in the kitchen.

Because of dyspraxia, I desperately require daily help with kitchen chores and other housework. The only humane way for CLSC (social services) to handle my case is to provide - at the very least - one hour of daily home care assistance. Instead, I'm forced to subsist on a terribly inadequate *one hour per week!*

In thinking about dyspraxia and all my suffering, it is difficult to fathom how my parents could have been so callous. If my "butterfingers" occasionally made a mess, it could have been blamed on carelessness; but when it occurred day-after-day and year-after-year with high frequency, their gross negligence was inexcusable.

Dr. Freedman once asked me which disorder gave me the most trouble. He was surprised when I didn't say autism and assured him that dyspraxia was the worst, by far!

CONCLUSION:
Because of Quebec's financial austerity, social services are virtually non-existent for autistic adults living on their own. Since dyspraxia is not recognized as a legitimate neurological disorder, it further reduces Marla's chances of getting the daily home care services, she must have. That she even gets one hour per week is a fluke!

The next chapter deals with abrasive textures that have Marla attacking them with venom.

18

Sensory Integration Disorder

INTRODUCTION:

Characteristic of many people with autism, Marla suffers from SID sensory integration disorder. A preponderance of mental health professionals do not understand SID or even believe it exists. Marla's psychiatrist for 33 years gave SID no more than "lip service," never acknowledging the countless ways it made her life a hellish experience.

If the sensory messages are not properly organized, integrated, and accurately processed in the brain - the feedback can produce an incorrect, even bizarre reaction. SID occurs when the brain misinterprets information coming from the senses: sight, sound, light, texture, smell, taste and stomach fullness.

Marla's SID is even more problematic when her brain fails to accurately process the *intensity* of a sensory stimulus; causing her to be, incorrectly, over-responsive or under-responsive in the way she reacts.

Text:
What may have been an early indication of SID, Mother recalled that in infancy I resisted being touched or cuddled by anyone. I would guess that either too much or too little stimulation would have caused a negative response; so that it needed to be given in ways acceptable to me. Apparently, these precautions were not taken and my aloofness remained intact. (See Chapter 3)

SID symptoms were ongoing throughout my Childhood and Teen Years. As an adult, it continues to affect my senses - mostly those involving sensitivity to touch, pain, bodily discomfort and physical contact with anyone. (See Chapter 1)

For proper responses, the brain has to first *accurately* absorb information coming to it from the several senses; with my SID, there are frequent *over-reactive distortions*. Then the stimulation of irritating, sensory inputs will cause angry responses - including destructive behavior.

For example, the textural corners and edges of paper have always irritated me. In first grade, the teacher noticed that I often mutilated paper. Blaming it on nothing more serious than naughty behavior, I was scolded whenever she saw me doing it. When I ripped paper to shreds with my teeth, classmates believed I ate the paper and made fun of me.

All my life, SID problems with paper have continued. The feel of paper bothers me a great deal. At work, the texture of bond paper, used in photocopying and laser printing, is the most bothersome; the handling of it causes me great stress. If a sheet is to be discarded, I tear it with gusto or rip it up with my teeth. In a batch of papers, the sight of a solitary edge sticking out makes me want to rip it off.

Whenever trying to locate misplaced papers at work or at home, I go berserk. Among the pile of clutter, if I grab some paper of no interest, I tear off the edges, crunch the remainder in a ball and throw it on the floor. If a specific edge or corner irritates my sense of touch, I am compelled to hack it on a hard surface with repeated blows until my anger is relieved. Had I tried to restrain myself, I'd feel drained and irritable.

To prevent my fingers from directly touching papers, I often enclose important ones in plastic; this allows me to further handle the documents without getting wrought-up. When writing on paper, I place a soft napkin under my hand to avoid direct contact.

In school, the girls had to wear long-sleeved blouses with uncomfortable collars and cuffs. Sensitive to textures, the fabric was an irritant that I viciously chewed. Mother would later become appalled at the damage and holler a blue streak!

On a similar note, years later, when I began working in a geriatric center as a nurse's aide, the required uniform was a source of irritation. If contact was made with my skin I responded with anger, ripping the fabric with my teeth.

My SID hatred for textures included the classroom desks in elementary school that I chewed, gnawed and defaced. In my room at home, I could not tolerate the feel of my desk and would attack it with my teeth. To prevent further damage, Father had it covered with a tough plastic laminate; yet seeing the wooden edges under the plastic were a visual irritant and I managed to chew them, nevertheless.

Beginning at age seven, Mother had me do kitchen chores that I hated. The surfaces and edges of kitchen counters and the feel of dish towels soon became biting and chewing targets. I especially loathed the chores because my Dyspraxia and SID caused them to be frustrating and intolerable. The ordinary dislike of kitchen tasks, by most kids, should not be confused with my extreme, all-consuming *anger* while doing them. (See Chapter 17)

As a young adult, I moved out of the family home. Then after living in two shoddy basement apartments, my parents helped me move into a high-rise, rental apartment. It was an improvement but soon my kitchen dysfunctions caused me to wreck the cabinets and counters. The landlord learned of the wreckage and threatened me with eviction, but since I paid to fix the damage and promised no more breakage, he was willing to give me a second chance. My kitchen SID continued with similar destruction or self-abuse no matter where I lived.

When having to prepare a meal, I seethe with ill temper. When beginning the chore, I am bothered by poor hand-eye coordination (dyspraxia); next comes the sensory discomforts of touch and sound, corrupted by my brain's SID.

I am unable to search for something in my purse and not touch the irritating fabric. Then there's a feeling of tactile rage; an overpowering need to destroy the handbag, ripping it apart with my teeth. Social workers have wondered about the need for destruction instead of simply, no longer using the handbag. I explained: "My hatred of the texture is so extreme that "attack and destroy" is the only feel-good response. Simply putting the offending purse away in a drawer would deny me the pleasure of biting, tearing and picking it to pieces!"

For me, dealing with paper is not solely a tactile problem. Also troublesome is the rustling sound of paper during a frenzied search, either at home or at work. I become irritated to the point where I must vocally mimic the crinkling noise, as a way of lessening stress. The sound mimicry I produce, during these rages, is a Tourette variant of my vocal tic. (See Chapter 6)

In fact, it is my SID habit to vocally mimic irritating sounds when doing hated chores, whether in the kitchen, tidying a purse or attempting to organize a chest of drawers.

Whenever kitchen utensils make noise by touching one another, it feels as though worms and bugs are crawling inside of me. My vocal imitations are then accompanied by fierce anger. These days, I restrain from wrecking the kitchen; instead, I wildly bite my arms, stomp the floor and scream. (See Chapter 11 – Self-Abuse)

Another type of mimicry, when working in the kitchen, is to imitate with hand motions the physical movements of objects falling on the floor or sliding in the sink.

I am also prone to SID motion sickness, due to the brain's inability to correctly process frequent changes in movement. Because of the many stops and starts, I cannot ride a city bus without feeling wretched from nausea.

With my fear of vomiting - an extreme phobia - I temperamentally *overreact* to any sickness that has the slightest chance of me throwing-up. (See Chapter 22 - Phobia and Migraines)

Similar to many people who get migraines and are prone to motion sickness, I am sensitive to bright lights, symptomatic of SID.

By having an SID gravity insecurity trait, it prevented me from doing amusement park rides or jumping off a swimming pool diving board. As for ice skating, since one's feet are not planted firmly on the ground, gravitational insecurity had kept me from learning to skate until I reached the ripe age of 31!

Because of extreme sensitivity to touch, pain and bodily discomfort, I find medical procedures intolerable. SID sensitivities reject contact with a physician - even being touched by one! An invasive medical procedure would result in sheer terror. The only one I endure is my yearly gynecology check-up when for months, prior to the exam, I tremble with apprehension.

With an extreme sensitivity to sound, my SID hates whiny songs, emotional music and love ballads. In the workplace, a co-worker played a weepy song that affected me so deeply, I hated it to the core of my being; a few lines of its obnoxious longing and unfulfilled desire festered in my brain. During the night, it caused bad dreams that awakened me early, sobbing and shedding copious tears!

Despite all the negatives, I find pleasure in several kinds of experiences related to the senses. There was always sensory enjoyment when having my arms, legs or back tickled by a family member. Magnets intrigue me when feeling their smoothness, hefting their weight and enjoying their forces of attraction and repulsion.

I've *fallen in love* with Furbaby, a unique blanket that an acquaintance gave me. Always on my bed, it is heavy and warm, made of fleece and has the tactile feel of soft fur. The blanket's main benefit is its wonderful touch. This is welcomed, even treasured, because so many entities in my life are loaded with unpleasant, even punishing textures. In bed, I stroke the blanket, talk to it like a pet, and I'm never without it, even during the summer! When the material folds over itself, it feels as though I have my arms around a furry animal, as though a live pet is snuggling up to me. Since I've never felt the least bit of cuddly love toward any other object, person or animal - I'm puzzled by what has become a perpetual attachment to Furbaby, a *positive* and *beneficial sensory overload.*

Because I must have the sense of inner fullness, I've always had a ravenous food appetite However, to keep my weight within the normal range I eat only low-calorie meals and endeavor to do vigorous, daily exercise.

My hindrances are living in Montreal with its miserable climate and deplorable food situation. Weather conditions prevent exercise half the year, while fresh produce and low-fat dairy items - at affordable prices - are hardly ever available.

Over-stimulation, when feeling rushed in the workplace, also worsens my SID condition. On days with too many responsibilities, I experience a sensory overload which lessens my efficiency.

For a lifetime, my senses have had a tendency to "come apart" with sadness and tears in response to life's many disappointments. There is also an inability to limit the duration of an emotion, causing me to continue with melancholy, long after the original stimulus is gone.

Topics related to death, destruction and mayhem affect me deeply. I avoid turmoil and sensationalism on TV because it throws me into a state of negative, sensory overload to a degree I am no longer able to function!

CONCLUSION:

Marla's lifelong sensory integration disorder is one of her most debilitating handicaps, affecting all the senses and is further complicated by its co-morbidity with Tourette and dyspraxia.

SID is given scant attention by neurological professionals, even less so, when it occurs in adults. Never, during her lifespan, has it seriously been addressed by any mental health professional, from whom she's sought counsel. Like dyspraxia, it is a disorder they believe may exist in childhood but is surely outgrown by maturity. On the contrary, Marla's SID has continued to worsen throughout her adult life.

Chapter 19 discusses Marla's unusual sensory connections.

19

Synaesthesia

INTRODUCTION:
The senses are functions of the mind, by which stimuli from outside or inside the body are perceived, as is the case with hearing, sight, smell, touch, taste, vibration, equilibrium and inner tension.

Synaesthesia is a neurological condition in which one type of stimulation evokes the sensation of an *additional* one, as when hearing a sound also produces the visualization of a color.

A synaesthesia commingling of the senses can occur in combination and with all manner of permutations, i.e with a sound, the person may not only *see* the color but also *taste* it.

Although, at times, it does happen under normal circumstances, stressful conditions tend to intensify Marla's synaesthesia. With much stress in preparing the evening meal, synaesthesia is a frequent occurrence. (See Chapter 11 – Kitchen Chores)

Text:
While always plagued by it, I first read of synaesthesia in 2004, analogous to "crossed wires" in the brain, affecting the nerves that process sensory information.

Numbers, letters, words, days of the week and so much more remind me of certain *colors*. When I was much younger, one reason big words used to interest me were the particular colors that came to mind when certain letter combinations appeared in my thoughts.

Even now, when I'm hearing or reading a particular word, number or letter of the alphabet I can experience all of the following: *see* a certain color, *see* a food having that color and also *taste* it. Therefore, an *auditory* or *visual* object can instantly bring forth, in my thinking, a repertoire of color, food and taste.

Immediately, after being exposed to any sound or stimulus that irritates me, there is a feeling of *inner tension*; it is similar to the inner tenseness of one's urge to do a Tourette tic. (See Chapter 6)

Listening to music can evoke images in my mind. I recall once *hearing* classical music that I perceived *visually* as the color brown.

One time, *listening* to a song, I kept *seeing* rows of curved lines.

I recall *listening* to a ballad and the singer's voice suggesting the *taste* of mozzarella cheese.

The *sound* made when a utensil slides in the kitchen sink gives my hand the feeling of *tactile* wetness.

Because of SID, I become irritated from abrasive *sounds* in the kitchen. Evoked are *visual* images of scratchy brushes with long, slender, pointed shapes. These false objects are often in reaction to the *sounds* of utensils in the sink sliding and bumping into one another, noises which my SID finds repulsive and abrasive. (See Sensory Integration Disorder - Chapter 18)

At times when hearing irritating *sounds*, weird inner *tactile* sensations are experienced but are difficult to explain. They are not quite the feeling of an ordinary itch, but more like a troubling itch that cannot be scratched, best described as the feeling of worms crawling inside of me. It typically occurs when I *see* or *hear* a utensil sliding in the sink.

Whenever doing kitchen chores with several senses activated simultaneously, it is an overwhelming experience that brings forth an emotional reaction of intense rage. It gets accompanied by my loud *vocal*, copycat mimicry of the *sounds* that most grate on my nerves.

Synaesthesia is overpowering; the result of vivid sensory illusions and the rapidity of occurrence. I'd give anything to be rid of this disorder, a misery that can violate any semblance of normal perception.

In discussing kitchen chores with Dr. Webster, my psychiatrist, I told him that an irritating *touch* can activate imaginary *visuals*, and visa-versa. Also, when preparing a meal, in order to release *inner tension* caused by synaethesia, my only option, since no longer smashing up the kitchen, is to savagely bite my arms. The self-abuse serves to relieve tension until the next enraged stimulus occurs, usually within a couple of minutes! Dr. Webster confirmed that it is not unusual for synaesthesia to interact with a sensory integration disorder. Actually, SID combined with synaesthesia, brings on the *visuals* and *touch* experiences responsible for much of my suffering.

CONCLUSION:
Marla's synaesthesia is an uncontrolled joining of senses. The *real information* of one sense is accompanied by an involuntary false perception in one, or more, additional senses. Each *involuntary* perception is often felt to be real, existing *outside* the body; instead, it is nothing more than *fantasy* in the mind's eye.

Marla wishes to be rid of synaesthesia, a loathsome disorder of suffering - climaxed by viciously biting her arms and in previous years the destruction of kitchens!

The next chapter describes a set of higher-order cognitive abilities in which Marla is deficient, these include: task persistence, behavioral planning, organizing ability, and freedom from distractibility.

20

Executive Function Disorder

INTRODUCTION:
The term "executive function" refers to the mental processes required in goal directed activity. These include the ability to start and terminate actions, to observe and change behavior as required, and figure out future plans when faced with tasks not done before. It also allows us to anticipate results and when necessary adapt to changed conditions.

Text:
According to the literature, many individuals on the autism spectrum have trouble with executive function; I am no exception. (See Chapter 2 - Autism)

As a person who operates by impulses, there is little, if any, executive function in my lifestyle. When wronged by someone, I *impulsively* strike back with verbal abuse. If healthful, reasonably priced food is not available at the supermarket, to lessen my frustration, I will *automatically* retaliate by damaging some junk food. (See Chapter 10 - Food Shopping)

When working in the library, I have difficulty screening-out distractions of irritating sounds coming from the adjacent corridor: women with clickety-clack heels, loud girlie talk, and whiny radio music coming from a room across the way. By complaining to my supervisor and suggesting that I be allowed to keep the door *closed*, but said without expressing myself with executive function skill, I failed to succeed in getting her cooperation.

Because of EFD executive function disorder, keeping my work area organized has never been possible; it is only with my supervisor's periodic help that my jumble of clutter gets systematized.

Without EF ability, I have trouble doing work projects in a logical sequence; it is the kind of judgment that often eludes me. When there is more than one task pending, and not been given exact dates and deadlines, I neither know which one to do first nor the best sequence to follow.

Should there be more than one method of doing something, I have an EFD problem in choosing the fastest and easiest way. Whether it's a chore at home or a problem at work, I have trouble weighing the pros and cons. Decisions! Decisions! The stumbling blocks cause stress and lost time. Keeping up with the job's increased responsibilities, yet always pushing myself to produce quality work, I suffer from Chronic Nervous Fatigue. (See Chapter 23)

Even with the handicap of EFD and multiple <u>neuro-disorders</u>*, my final work output is always completed on schedule, albeit problems along the way. I have the advantage of living within walking distance of the library and when necessary, I return in the evening to finish whatever needs to be done. There is a price to pay because, at the very least, a portion of the extra time expended could have been saved, had it been done with skilled pre-planning.

EFD also affects my personal life. A year ago, my father asked me to do him a favor and decipher the manual that came with his videocassette recorder. Having the booklet in my possession and despite reminders from him, I procrastinated for nine months! Finally, gritting my teeth and forcing myself, on a day he was away, I went to his house and with the manual in hand, worked through the instructions and got his VCR functioning.

Admittedly, I am bothered when it comes to doing anything new or difficult, always craving simplicity and the familiar. This EFD trait also applies to personal tasks. I shun unexpected paperwork arriving in the mail plus the miscellaneous directives from the condo office; whenever possible, I prevail on my father to take care of them.

With poor EFD, I also have a problem heeding oral directives. For example, when Father gives me a ride to the store or downtown to the psychiatrist's office, he tells me where to meet him for the trip home. Because my mind is racing with extraneous thoughts, what he says rarely sinks in and I don't usually wait for him in the right place. He then expresses wonderment: "How can a daughter so intelligent be so stupid!"

If I'm talking with someone, EFD can affect the interacting process in two ways. Firstly, I have trouble with impulse control. When someone begins to ask a question or make a statement, I often blurt out my own thoughts before he has a chance to finish.

Secondly, while the other person is talking, my mind is often kept busy with extraneous topics. Based on my own racing thoughts, I will make a comment that has little, or nothing, to do with the topic at hand. With poor impulse control, I have a need to express my own thoughts and, frankly, have little, or no, interest in what the other person has to say.

Other than a disorganized area at work, there is my pocketbook full of junk and an apartment always in disarray. With so much clutter, I expend half my life looking for things!

Because of EFD, while in the midst of doing a home chore that I'm intent on finishing, I can easily get distracted without even realizing it. For example, I may be straightening out a massive accumulation of papers on the living room table, but unexpectedly come upon an undone crossword puzzle. Without thinking, I easily get absorbed in doing the crossword.

In deciding what to eat for each meal, my ironbound routine spares me from having to make choices. This is one function when having an executive function disorder does not become an issue. To the greatest extent possible, each successive day of the week specifies a certain meal, or if the exact same food is not available, ones that are similarly equivalent in type and calories, usually suffice.

The only break in the food routine is once a year when I join Father for a Chinese meal to celebrate my birthday!

CONCLUSION:
Marla's neurology is defective in executive function ability, causing her personal life and job performance to be terribly inefficient and stressful.

EFD also plays havoc with higher-level cognitive abilities, such as: self-regulation, prioritization of work, awareness of time, abstract reasoning, logical analysis, and making plans with flexibility.

There is no cure for EFD.

The following chapter deals with the interesting topic of co-mobidity; how specific disorders "join forces" and cause the end result to be more severe.

21

Co-morbid and Invisible

INTRODUCTION:
In the context of Marla's neurological disorders, co-morbidity is the existence of traits - from two or more disorders - acting in synergy*.

Throughout her life, several co-morbid neurological conditions have caused significant dysfunctions in her learning ability, physical adeptness, social interaction, mood adjustment, and thought patterns.

Since brain disorders are invisible to the naked eye, co-workers who know Marla cannot fathom her unproductive life style, she being a person of outstanding intelligence.

Text:
What bothers me is that people expect much more from me than I can achieve. They confuse my computer ability and other workplace skills with those of someone who is an all-around, well-adjusted person - capable of doing most anything he or she wishes.

One reason for this misconception is that my severe Autism, Attention Deficit Disorder, Sensory Integration Disorder and other co-morbid afflictions are debilitating - within my brain - but not seen by the human eye. People may notice my lack of sociality and eccentricities but otherwise consider me a highly intelligent person who, in their mindset, is capable of doing most anything, if willing to make the effort. (See Chapters 2, 5 and 18, respectively.)

My slew of <u>neuro-disorders</u>*, invisible to persons around me, has a devastating influence on my emotional health. It sets up an environment of misunderstanding, doubt, and even denial regarding the validity of my several dysfunctions. People need to understand that it is normal to appear okay on the *outside* but have hardwired, impaired functioning on the *inside*.

In a similar vein, both my parents, for a lifetime, have been in *disbelief* regarding the existence of my neurological condition - invisible to the naked eye. They've denied me a lifetime of acceptance and much needed support; unable to reconile high intelligence with my invisible disorders. Their denial, of the latter, has never wavered.

People see me as someone who finds endless excuses to justify my rejection of what the culture has to offer: hobbies for enjoyment and intellectual interests for personal growth. Having no awareness of my neurological baggage, they jump to conclusions and depict me as a lazy underachiever.

A few of my "invisible disabilities" are not that *invisible*. Because of Dyspraxia (See Chapter 17) others will often notice my abnormal body movements and clumsy hands. Lacking dexterity is not seen as a neuro-disability, as would a malformed leg or twisted arm; instead, people believe my clumsy hands and peculiar gait are situational and with conscientious effort, could be much improved. I also suffer a disservice when compared with a preponderance of other <u>HFA</u>* individuals who have made a far better life adjustment. The discrepancy may lie in the fact most HFA's have considerably fewer and less severe co-morbid disorders.

Society's work ethic teaches that adults who are *seemingly* able-bodied, with normal intelligence, are obliged to be self-sufficient and not seek assistance from others, unless on a paid basis. In contrast, if I had serious disorders that were visually obvious, society might show understanding and perhaps be supportive.

As for the root cause of many severe, neuro-disorders, I believe that multiple brain areas may have been damaged during gestation - the result of hormone injections Mother had been taking to facilitate her pregnancy with me. (See Chapter 3)

A co-morbid disorder will naturally bring on a more extreme behavior than a disorder acting in solo. My disorders that may interact with co-morbidity, include the following:

  *Attention Deficit Disorder/Hyperactivity (ADD/H)

  *Autism

  *Migraines

  *Dyspraxia

  *Sensory Integration Disorder (SID)

  *Passive-Aggressive Personality Disorder (PAPD)

  *Oppositional Defiant Disorder (ODD)

  *Borderline Personality Disorder (BP)

  *Synaesthesia

  *Executive Function Disorder (EFD)

  *Prosopagnosia - (Face Blindness)

  *Vomiting Phobia

  *Chronic Nervous Fatigue

*Tourette Syndrome (TS)

Mental health professionals are, oftentimes, expert in specific neurological disorders but lack the ability to comprehensively treat patients having multiple dysfunctions. The sheer number of my co-morbid disorders is profound. My Psychiatrist, of more than 30 years, while an expert in autism, lacked sufficient background to deal with the wide extent of my co-morbid dysfunctions. (See Chapter 14)

It should by noted, however, that Sensory Integration Disorder and Dyspraxia (if recognized at all) are not the kinds of dysfunctions ordinarily treated by psychiatrists, and more within the province of OT *. (See Chapters 18 and 17, respectively.)

With autism, Dr. Freedman's specialty, he would downplay other neurological disorders affecting my HFA behaviors. For example, it is autism that basically causes my behavioral Inflexibility; however, two other disorders, Tourette Syndrome and Borderline Personality, acting in concert, will determine *ways* in which the inflexibility gets expressed, yet hardly get mentioned by him. (See Chapters 29, 6 and 32, respectively.)

Any substitutions in my personal routines are not acceptable. If what I depend on for usual satisfaction is not forthcoming, my inflexibility in co-morbidity with a Passive Aggressive Personality puts me in a "revenge-like" state of mind. For example, if I go to a supermarket seeking reasonably priced low-calorie yogurt and the only alternative is a junky, high-fat, sugary product - a few of the store's yogurt containers end up with no refrigeration and missing their lids. My caper of retribution gives me a feeling of satisfaction and also a welcome Tourette release of tension. (See Chapter 33)

When overwhelmed in preparing a meal, I furiously bite my hands and arms; the self-abuse can be blamed on a co-morbid mix of autism, dyspraxia, sensory integration disorder, synaesthesia and Tourette.

While therapists refer to a neurological disorder as a single entity, it is rarely that clear-cut; certainly in my case, multiple disorders usually work in synergy to actualize my social misconduct.

I suffer from a pervasive and stressful anxiety. Any visualization method, bent on teaching me how to relax, requires an imagination that is blocked and prevented by my autism.

By also having a co-morbid Attention Deficit Disorder, any prolonged focusing of paying attention is well-nigh impossible. (See Chapters 7 and 5, respectively.) So for the above reasons visualization therapy is impossible; my only release from anxiety is deep sleep.

Two traits of autism deal with *harm avoidance* and *inflexibility*, integral components of my lifestyle.

When reaching adulthood, the Tourette tics become less frequent but transfer into a trait of *weak impulse control*. For example, TS acts in synergy with Passive Aggressive Behavior and "pushes" me into frequent vandalizing. (See Chapter 33)

Typical HFA individuals, express a wish for human relationships. They tend to persevere, though lacking social skills plus finding people involvement stressful. I march to a different drummer! My HFA is co-morbid with schizoid personality* traits that preclude any need for human friendship. I am a true loner who requires a solitary existence, has never bonded with anyone, nor have the desire to do so.

CONCLUSION:
As to the ongoing misery of Marla's daily life struggle, other people have little awareness. Because her outward appearance is essentially normal and her brain function disorders mostly invisible, co-workers and others do not provide any psychological or tangible support, even though Marla is in great need.

With a personality complex of severe co-morbidity and virtually no support, she can no longer live in a city that only adds to her misery. Montreal does not begin to meet her needs for daily outdoor biking, affordable low-calorie food, human civility, and adequate municipal services. Her greatest wish is relocating to a small city with a hot, dry climate, offering several of the plus factors now missing in her life.

In Chapter 22, Marla copes with two situational stressors: a vomiting phobia and migraine headaches.

22

Vomiting Phobia and Migraine Headaches

INTRODUCTION:
A phobia is not unusual for those having Tourette Syndrome. Throughout her life, Marla has suffered from both a vomiting phobia and Tourette. (See Chapter 6)

Her migraine headaches are known to occur during times of unusual stress, often activated by Marla's difficulties in the workplace. (See Chapter 26 - Medical Library Assistant)

Text:
Vomiting is my only phobia and one of the greatest fears in my life. Everything about it terrifies me: the explosiveness, loud sounds, awful sight, terrible smell and loss of control. My earliest memory of vomiting goes back to age 5 when I had stomach flu, accompanied by nausea and throwing-up.

Because of having an extreme responsiveness to all *bodily discomforts*, a volunteer community worker once suggested that my Sensory Integration Disorder may have contributed to the uncontrollable severity of my vomiting phobia. (See Chapter 18)

There was also a stomach flu at age 6 when I up-chucked twice; since then, I've had no additional vomiting. Yet etched in memory, I will never forget the foul-tasting vomit traveling from my stomach, up through the esophagus and then straight out my mouth! There were other stomach flu attacks over the years, accompanied by nausea but having learned to avoid food completely - I was able to prevent any future vomiting.

During a conversation, ordinary people react to my phobia the same way they react to my aversion for housework: they smile and don't take it seriously. They typically say that I'm no different than anyone else because nobody likes either of those things. What people fail to realize is that my *not liking* something is quite different from experiencing sheer terror at the very thought of it; no crisis in my life could ever be more traumatic than vomiting!

My sister Sherry was prone to having migraines. I now believe that many of her sudden vomiting bouts were caused by the onset of migraine attacks.

Although Sherry vomited from most sicknesses, there were times I had no clue that she even had an illness. We shared a bedroom and sometimes during the night, I'd suddenly get awakened by her frantic dash to the toilet, followed by explosive vomiting noises. Affected so deeply, I would often regress to infantile rocking in my bed and sobbing - absolutely terrified! Even now, decades later, just recalling the sounds of Sherry's nightly escapades, I still respond with fearful disgust and loathing!

Aware of my childhood phobia, Father was most considerate. When Sherry had tonsillitis, along with stomach ailments and accompanied by vomiting - he took me for drives just to get me out of the house. In that regard, he had far more empathy than did my mother.

Once in our early teens, knowing I had an irrational fear of vomiting, Sherry teased me during one of her migraines, by eating lots of junk food to deliberately make herself throw-up. In a state of horror, I raced down into the basement, remaining there until I could be sure her despicable prank was over.

The summer when I was age 8, with no school and lots of time on my hands, I had a preoccupation with vomiting; that was accompanied by psychosomatic stomach pains. I could not stop obsessing about it. Every few minutes, I kept asking Mother: "Will I soon vomit?" She became enraged with the endless questioning, and finally bellowed: "I am going to stick my finger down your nose and then you'll know exactly how it feels to vomit!" That was no way to treat a daughter with a vomiting phobia. While "down your nose" made no sense, it terrified me nevertheless!

During stomach flu season when the bug starts making its rounds, I become more unsociable than usual. Whether in the workplace, on the street or in food stores, I am forever darting away from anyone getting too close!

There is a form of Behavior Modification for treating my vomiting phobia. The first step is learning to do relaxation exercises; a reason I once got involved with techniques of Relaxation therapy. Unfortunately, my Attention Deficit impairment did not allow for the necessary mind-set of learning how to relax. As a result and with great disappointment, I was prevented from using behavior mod as a treatment for the phobia. (See Chapters 16, 8 and 5, respectively.)

The other treatment possibility would have been desensitization, which exposes the client to whatever she is fearful of. In my case, introducing small amounts of the foul substance would have been unacceptable - a terrifying procedure, I could not have tolerated.

Migraines run in my family and I started having them at age 18. They can be triggered by stress, anxiety, a change in routine, power outages, severe weather or any upsetting incident.

The migraines often start with a mental warning called an <u>aura</u>*, usually with zigzag lights that gradually expand and then disappear. Nothing can rid oneself of the aura until it leaves on its own, usually after 15 to 20 minutes.

An aura is the most upsetting phase of the migraine, because I'm *seeing* something that I know does not exist; however, it is a blessing in disguise; since it gives me enough time to take some painkiller for the headache and <u>Gravol</u>* to stave off any nausea.

With the increased stressors of this millennium, migraine attacks are more frequent. If there are multiple ones during the week, I walk around in a cantankerous mood, displaying a degree of rudeness that others don't understand.

CONCLUSION:

Marla's vomiting phobia embodies an intense fear that compels her to avoid coming down with stomach flu and throwing up. If infected with the bug, she abstains from eating food until the flu period is over and no likelihood of vomiting.

During a migraine when the aura begins, she immediately takes medications to avoid any occurrence of nausea and its precursor to vomiting.

For Marla, there is neither an acceptable treatment to rid her of the phobia nor any preventative for having migraines.

The next chapter puts Marla in a condition of physical and mental burnout.

23

Chronic Nervous Fatigue

INTRODUCTION:
CNF Chronic nervous fatigue emanating from the central nervous system is highly debilitating. It is made more dysfunctional when multiple neuro-disorders* act in synergy.

As a result of Marla's CNF, she has reduced ability to meet the demands of daily life. The disorder is symptomatic of extreme tiredness that limits the amount of time she is able to function at her job in the library. Part time work, four mornings a week is virtually all the energy she can muster. In addition to the inevitable fatigue, there is concurrent short-term memory loss.

Text:
When clobbered, all at once, by my boss with an excessive number of tasks to be done, I find it terribly draining on my nervous system. In addition, any of the work requiring inordinate focus and concentration becomes overtaxing.

Getting a good night's rest and waking up refreshed does not sufficiently revitalize my nervous system. There has been a cumulative effect of both my stressful job and the debilitating chores at home. One might compare my mental acuity depletion to a longstanding, gradual "cerebral burnout;" it has gotten progressively worse, to an extent, no longer sufficiently alleviated by deep sleep.

Cerebral burnout affects many more <u>HFA</u>* adults than the mental health community is willing to acknowledge. With the media publicizing only the autism success stories, the public does not realize that most autistic individuals withstand inordinate stress in holding down a job; when factoring in personal responsibilities, chronic nervous fatigue is often the result!

Countless HFA adults, trying to persevere in the mainstream, are not getting help from family, friends and mental health professionals. And are not receiving support that would facilitate better functioning, despite autism. For successful employment, what is required is a set of responsibilities, not overwhelming, that an HFA can handle without succumbing to burnout.

There are mental health professionals and social services personnel who believe the best lifestyle for an HFA is to *maximize* their responsibilities, expecting them to eventually reach a full stage of normal life adjustment. With chronic nervous fatigue and burnout - often the result - excessive responsibility has been proven wrong!

My father has a hard time understanding how my white collar, part-time job - in a library - can be so enervating. I try to explain that working in the library does not require physical stamina, but does necessitate excessive demands on my nervous energy. Though not physically tired, I become *mentally* exhausted.

Plus, there are other factors: Brain overload of nervous fatigue occurs because in addition to my library job, there is also food shopping, meal preparation, housekeeping and self-care; so that I often feel rushed, overwhelmed and depleted of energy.

With my *hell on earth* difficulty in doing kitchen chores, there are inevitable spills, messes and breakage; so that my nervous fatigue is sure to be a daily occurrence. (See Chapter 11 - Kitchen Chores) All of my stressors* incapacitate the *same* central nervous system; some of my fiercest kitchen rages occur on days when because of deadlines, I've already put in extra hours at work; a cumulative effect that becomes overwhelming!

Most people with disabilities, severe as mine, are not employed but live on public assistance. I believe that years of forcing myself to hold down a stressful job has permanently enfeebled my CNS*; with my extreme fatigue now occurring *sooner* in the day, it feels as though I've been beaten to a pulp!

When starting to prepare the evening meal, Dyspraxia makes it impossible to do the chores properly. In struggling with my uncoordinated hands, the day's nervous fatigue worsens, and I'm stuck with foul-ups due to clumsy hands and poor Sensory Integration. All of my frustration tolerance is soon gone and full of rage; I begin to wildly bite my arms and behave like a mental case! (See Chapters 17 and 18, respectively.)

Responsibilities at work and doing chores at home are not the whole story. Adding to my energy depletion is the stress of being stuck in the mainstream of an abrasive, overcrowded city and assaulted by a cacophony of foreign languages. All of this bedlam is unnerving and takes its toll on my nervous system.

The fall and spring months are confusing, because the weather can fluctuate with changes throughout the day. Since the temperatures are transitional, my nervous system gets "confused" and I can feel warm one minute and cold the next; as a result, the Montreal climate adds to my CNF.

All types of stress conditions will further exhaust my nervous system: a power outage, a thunderstorm, severe weather, an appliance failure, a serious quarrel, lack of Exercise, unaffordable Food, and much more. (See Chapters 12 and 10)

In addition, daily crises that suggest thoughts of The Quickening are part and parcel of my nervous fatigue. (See Chapter 34)

Since the 1990's, my chronic nervous fatigue has gradually worsened. It is the result of having struggled for years in the mainstream where I do not belong. In fact, what used to be nervous system fatigue is fast becoming my *nervous system* <u>*burnout*</u>*.

I am sensing the same "end of life" tiredness that can impact old people. Though I just turned 50, there is growing CNF and a feeling of not having much to live for: fed up with what life has to offer!

Compared to other HFA clients, whose CNF actually improved as they received psychotherapy, Dr. Freedman (Psychiatrist) could not understand why my condition was getting progressively worse. What may have caused a lack of progress was his focus on my autism; while he gave scant attention to the other disorders affecting my poor my life adjustment, i.e. dyspraxia, sensory integration disorder, and lots more. (See Chapter 14)

Another possible reason for the seeming uniqueness of my condition is because most other people with severe HFA, comparable to mine, do not have to struggle with the disadvantages of an independent life, fending for themselves. Their nerves do not accumulate mental fatigue, because they lead simpler lives and are possibly cared for in a family setting, a <u>group home</u>* or <u>assisted living</u>*.

In discussing my nervous fatigue disability, somebody might question how I have the energy to do exercise, such as cycling miles on my bike, climbing Mt. Royal, ice skating and rollerblading when my nervous system easily tires from responsibilities done at work and chores done at home. There is an explanation for the seeming inconsistency: Vigorous sports require physical stamina which primarily depend on the heart, lungs, and muscles - which for me function normally; so that my nervous system plays only a minor role when doing a physical workout. For example, riding a bicycle requires intact mental functioning to maintain balance and coordination of movements, but once having mastered the process, it became automatic and effortless. While I may get physically tired from biking several miles, I am never mentally drained.

The workplace job and home chores that I struggle with are not physically strenuous; rather, they suffer from chronic nervous fatigue. These are brain disorders with over-burdened neuron circuits; they may get worn out, due to overuse and aging.

Even when I cram too many worthwhile pursuits into a day, I experience the same nervous fatigue. My CNS can only cope with a limited number of activities and they need to be spaced with intervals of relaxation.

When my nervous fatigue gets maxed out, a good meal does not revitalize it. To experience any sense of renewal, which is limited at best, requires a period of deep sleep. (See Chapter 12 - Oblivion)

If I had a homemaker to prepare the evening meal, it would alleviate a major source of chronic fatigue; affecting an already overtaxed nervous system of job stress and the day's happenings.

As for government aid, a sudden brain trauma accident causing acute nervous system fatigue may qualify the person to receive financial assistance. But since my condition is inborn, invisible and difficult to prove - a disability pension may never be forthcoming.

While Dr. Freedman believed my need for the pension was genuine and deserving, he was convinced that applying for it would be a wasted effort. As they say in baseball, "three strikes and you're out", specifically: my holding down a part-time job, owning a condominium apartment (due to parental financial aid), and Quebec's austerity program.

CONCLUSION:

Mental <u>stressors</u>* in the workplace, the chores at home, and life in an abrasive city - cumulatively - place severe limitations on Marla's exceptionally fragile central nervous system. Unless ongoing tangible support, somehow, becomes a lifestyle reality, the outcome for Marla will be a continuation of nervous fatigue, leading to burnout.

Next are three deficiencies that sabotage Marla's interpersonal functioning.

24

Theory of Mind, Humor and Faces

INTRODUCTION:
Often at odds with what the other person is verbalizing, "theory of mind" is the ability to surmise the individual's true mind set or intentions; it is knowledge gleaned from facial expression and body language. Marla is lacking theory of mind, symptomatic of autism.

As with most autistic individuals, she is without a sense of humor. Marla can neither generate her own comical remarks nor understand the humor expressed by others. Whatever makes an anecdote amusing is lost on Marla. She often interprets a person's joke in a literal sense, word-for-word, until otherwise corrected.

She is a victim of face blindness (prosopagnosia); an inability or difficulty to recognize familiar faces.

Text:
Poor theory of mind has always affected communication with my parents. An acquaintance, told me that the dire warnings they dished out, said to me in anger, were no more than idle threats. One example was a threatening scare tactic to *disown me* if I smashed up the kitchen in my fine condo; a new apartment made possible with

their financial assistance. Although only a scare tactic, it was a cruel thing to say. Confused and fearful, I could not help but take their bluff and bluster literally. (I later learned that people with normal theory of mind can differentiate valid threats from empty ones, while autistics in lacking that ability, are unable to make the distinction.) (See Chapter 11)

It was wrong to use that tactic on a daughter with autism. Parents and others should say exactly what they mean - especially when using figures of speech that can be taken literally.

I was told by the supervisor of <u>CLSC</u>* that some workers who had provided homecare assistance were *afraid* of me. It was because I had mentioned biting my arms, out of anger and frustration, when doing kitchen chores! At the time, the workers did not seem upset; I have to believe it was poor theory of mind which prevented me from recognizing, what must have been their obvious, disapproving facial expressions.

My dislike of reading novels is also related to an inadequate theory of mind. Characters interact in novels just as people do in real life. The reader needs to surmise inner motives that may be in conflict with what is being said. Not liking people stories also reflects my aversion for humanity - whether novels, magazines, movies or TV.

Throughout my life, there were family jokes that went over my head, causing me to feel confused and anxious. For example, I did not understand someone saying, in a moment of levity: "I tiptoed past the medicine cabinet, afraid of waking up the sleeping pills." Because sleeping pills are inanimate objects, the supposed joke made no sense to me, yet it produced laughter from everyone else; as the family oddball, I felt stupid!

When Mother once said: "I laughed so hard, I was beside myself," I could not fathom how a person could be in "two places" at the same time. To avoid her inevitable "put down," I did not question it.

In my early teens, I decided to learn a sense of humor - believing it was an important skill required in social situations. Therefore, I began reading joke books and committed some of the humor to memory. Neither effort was successful; nobody laughed at my humor and I found the project extremely boring!

As a teenager, still living at home, taking my cue from a comedy on TV, I attempted a prank at Mother's expense to make her look foolish. My "joke" was inserting a straight pin in a ball of clay that she was about to use for modeling. Even though she noticed the pin before getting stuck by it, she angrily accused me of having done a "sick joke." Only trying to be funny, I considered her anger undeserved and hurtful! However, I began to realize that practical jokes or reciting contrived jokes, with poor delivery, were neither funny nor of interest to anyone. And it became obvious, to me, that a sense of humor was an inborn, natural ability which I simply didn't have.

When I was 11, my sister Sherry concocted a made-up story that I had been adopted. Unable to detect her attempt at a practical joke, the idea upset me so much my face began to tic furiously. I was enraged at the thought of being adopted; and to think, they never even told me! (See Chapter 6 - Tourette)

Mother explained that my sister was only joking and assured me that I was not adopted. I felt a sense of relief. Nevertheless, I still got a tongue-lashing for what she said were my "ugly facial tics," even though uncontrollable.

I have trouble recognizing faces and there is no cure for face blindness. A person is insulted when I fail to acknowledge their greeting; I recall my embarrassment when I mistook an individual for someone else and greeted her with the wrong name! Nowadays, I tell new acquaintances about my face blind disorder; so they will understand and not be offended if I snub them or get them confused with somebody else.

In watching a TV medical drama, I get characters with similar faces mixed up. I can see their individual facial features, but lack the ability to see the parts *interacting* as a totality and be able to recognize the entire face. By mixing-up the characters, I often lose track of the story.

When someone greets me, I cannot always be sure who I'm talking to. I find that face blindness and my poor short-term memory go hand-in-hand. At the large nursing home where I work, there is considerable turnover of staff; I find it all very confusing. Often, after several encounters, I am able to recognize an individual; then if he or she leaves and is replaced by someone new, I'm back to learning another face.

CONCLUSION:

Lacking theory of mind, Marla is mostly clueless in her ability to understand other people's actions, beliefs, attitudes, intentions and emotions. Individuals around her can seem incoherent and unintelligible. Unless it's a medical topic, diversions such as novels and motion pictures - with social situations - are usually avoided because they are poorly understood and of no interest.

A sense of humor, not inborn, has always eluded Marla; a social skill she very much wished to have. When in conversation, various laughter will often puzzle her and she has to wonder: "Are they laughing at me or something else."

Unless there's an unusual feature about a person's looks, it often requires several encounters before the face is etched as a totality in Marla's memory.

In the next chapter, Marla discusses the circumstances of having been a nurse's aide and her demotion to cleaning lady.

25

Nurse's Aide and Housekeeper

INTRODUCTION:
At age 18, Marla began working as a nurse's aide in a geriatric, long-term care institution. Since her mother was employed there as a secretary and well regarded, Marla was hired without the usual interview and for a job which required no formal training. Her responsibilities were to assist nurses in caring for the elderly and chronically ill patients.

Worried that Marla had never been a "people-person," Mrs. Comm believed that she would learn proper social behavior while interacting with nurses, co-workers, elderly patients and visitors.

Text:
Mother easily got me the job as nurse's aide because she had influence with people in the administration. In the initial orientations, I had trouble learning the basic procedures, modeled for me by staff people - a stumbling block since I could never learn anything by imitation. Difficulties with my poor hand-eye coordination were yet another hindrance, see Chapter 17 - Dyspraxia.

My uniform's texture was a constant irritant; I picked, chewed and tore at the fabric. (See Chapter 18 - Sensory Integration Disorder)

Most of the work seemed impossible, but in time I was able to manage personal care tasks, such as bathing patients and also learned how to use the Hoyer Lift, a mechanical device for lifting patients that I very much enjoyed doing.

It got to the point, I was not interested in any aspect of patient care except those dependent on the lift. It was used to maneuver a bed patient into a wheel chair and then later back into bed; those tasks elated me! Whenever possible, I'd refuse an assignment if the patient's daily routine did not require using the device.

As for the elderly who were ambulatory and did not depend on the machine but needed only nursing care, those individuals positively bored me! I would then prevail upon another aide to take my patient in exchange for her sedentary patient, requiring the lift.

For safety, it was mandated that the lift be operated by two aides; a regulation I disobeyed by haranguing the scheduled aide and argued my way out of working in tandem. When confronted with a co-worker who would not break the rule, I would either refuse the assignment or wait until she went on break, then behind her back I was able to use the lift, unescorted by her.

Because of so much insubordination, I should have been fired; but surprisingly the lift obsession, by itself, never got me into serious trouble.

As an inflexible person, I was hooked on that model device and *only* that one; nothing else would suffice! To my disappointment, in the early eighties, the Hoyer Lift was replaced by a new model; causing me to lose all interest in what had become an unrelenting obsession.

Being a nurse's aide provided ample opportunities to obtain food for my low-calorie diet and satisfy my voracious appetite.

Feeding patients in their rooms with nobody else around, I snitched a spoonful of their vegetable from each tray and when they finished eating, I would also pocket the leftovers. Though never caught in the act of doing it, one day my stash was revealed to a supervisor; it was wrapped in a paper towel and leaking from my pocket! All I got was a reprimand for taking leftovers from the patients' trays *after* they had eaten. I lucked out that she didn't know it included food I'd swiped *before* they had eaten.

The kitchen help would occasionally give me untouched, perfectly good food. At other times, when they were on break, I'd sneak into the kitchen and "liberate" half-used containers of cottage cheese and diet jam but would never steal the unopened ones.

Early some mornings, I noticed the kitchenette had been left unlocked where the night staff food was kept. Seeing no one around, I would doggy-bag leftover salads, vegetables and dairy. One morning I noticed the door closed but with a key in the lock. Removing the key, I took it to a nearby locksmith, had a duplicate made, kept the copy, and replaced the original. Future mornings, with my own key and nobody watching, I had easy access and never got caught! Since it was food meant for the night staff and only leftovers were taken, I didn't suffer any guilt pangs!

When I was subsequently demoted to Housekeeping, with its shift beginning an hour later, my little caper no longer felt safe. By that time, there were people circulating in the area and the danger of getting caught!

Believing that some staff were supportive and could be trusted, I freely discussed my personal problems including the bad relationship with my mother and the struggle in learning to be an aide. A few of them friendly with Mother, squealed and also told her about my chewed-up uniform, the lift obsession, odd food habits, inability to get along with co-workers, poor job performance and how I sat not crossing my legs in the cafeteria, with underpants showing!

Full of venom, Mother ordered me to stop betraying family secrets and learn proper decorum in the workplace. Otherwise, I'd be fired from the job and disowned by her! After that, I tried to keep my mouth shut, but my obvious misbehaviors were still reported to her.

On a busy day, one of my patients was scheduled for a bath. Other aides and orderlies also had baths to give. Since we each had to wait our turn to use one of the two tubs, I was in no mood for a long delay on line. So very early in the day, ahead of the others, I securely strapped my patient in a bath chair and wheeled her to the tub room. I thought it was safe to leave her alone and since she was a submissive individual, I was certain that she'd sit still. Planning to leave her unsupervised for a few minutes, I went to the nurse's station to hear the daily shift report. Suddenly, one of the staff came running in to tell us that she found my patient lying on the floor with her safety belt undone. Even though she suffered no injury, I got into serious trouble leaving her unattended.

The head nurse, who already hated my guts, urged the nursing director to have me fired from a job I'd held for eight years. In response, the director called me a non-functioning person, ordered me off the premises and had me suspended without pay.

I went home in tears. A co-worker, knowing what happened, contacted the union. Subsequently, I was allowed to return but prohibited from any contact with patients. As a learning experience, I was ordered to accompany one of the aides and observe her for a week of orientation; it was all very degrading, but after that I was permitted to work on my own.

Then, a few days later, I received a letter from the nursing director terminating my employment. It formally stated that I had no sensitivity for the needs of elderly patients and should not be allowed to work with them. The shock of her letter caused my state of mind to have a severe Emotional Meltdown, see Chapter 7.

Believing I should *not* be fired, the union fought on my behalf and had the dismissal overturned, so that I continued as a nurse's aide.

The nursing home administration, however, was not to be outma-neuvered. Using psychological harassment, every few days I was lectured by a different member of management telling me I was unfit for nurse's aide work, no good at relating to patients, would do better working with "things," and suggested I transfer into House-keeping. His statement, though cruel, was true since all my life I've had no genuine feeling for people.

The bath chair incident was still being held against me, so that I was being closely monitored.

As time progressed, management along with staff on my floor became increasingly dissatisfied with my frequent inflexibility, manipulative behavior, and unwillingness to follow directives. For example, I refused going to early lunch and insisted on the late lunch hour, every day. Adding fuel to the fire, a few aides falsely accused me of stealing clothes from their patients.

A clique of nurse's aide co-workers acted supportive and seemed extremely nice. I soon discovered it was all make-believe. Seeing me panic one morning, when my purse had been stolen, they clapped their hands and howled with laughter. That was the final straw. Not able to withstand any more hostility and setbacks, I capitulated and requested a transfer to Housekeeping.

Because the head nurse on my floor had a reputation for being unfair and even irrational, Mother was supportive. She also considered the director's letter and harassment by management a defamation of character, and even suspected the original incident was not my fault; she believed I might have been framed - that someone unbuckled the safety belt to get me fired.

As for the transfer to Housekeeping, Mother knew it would be a boring and demeaning job, and she began soliciting management to find me a better position somewhere in the institution.

Being rid of the nursing department's harassment and not having to deal with nasty co-workers, my transfer to Housekeeping was at first a welcome relief.

I no longer had access to food from patients' meal trays but lucked-out with a new source of free edibles. In the pot-washer room, located in the basement, I would doggy bag leftover vegetables, hard boiled eggs and cottage cheese - whatever coincided with my healthful diet.

Since I was forced to work with trashy equipment, the job presented problems. The vacuum cleaner had poor suction and when changing the flimsy dust bag, it easily tore open with the contents spilling onto my uniform and the dust choking me!

As with all my clumsy attempts at cleaning, my Dyspraxia of poor hand-eye coordination made the work even more frustrating. (See Chapter 17)

I began hating both the job and the supervisor, a taskmaster who treated me like a robot, expecting non-stop work just as the union rep had warned me. She would time the rest periods and dock my pay if I spent an extra minute on break; having become sheer drudgery the work was intolerable.

Aside from the boredom and filth, the job was repulsive. Many of the patients spat phlegm and spittle everywhere, including the ash trays for me to clean; I began refusing to do any chore so disgusting!

Becoming more-and-more fed up with the job, I increasingly called in sick with invented illnesses. Mother was supportive and reimbursed any lost salary. My <u>situational depression</u>* caused by the housekeeping job was a source of concern to the union officials and also the institution's health nurse.

All the while my mother bugged the administration to find me work that was more suitable. I'm not sure who accomplished the feat, whether it was my mother, the health nurse, the union or their combined effort; but I was assigned to work, on a trial basis, as an assistant in the hospital's medical library.

CONCLUSION:
Being a nurse's aide was a people-intensive job, totally at odds with Marla's asocial personality.

As a highly intelligent person doing menial, repetitive work in Housekeeping the job became increasingly unsuitable and repugnant.

In spring 1986, Marla began working in the hospital medical library for a few hours, one day a week, while continuing in Housekeeping the rest of the time. As she successfully learned additional library tasks, the hours were gradually increased. By fall of 1989, Marla was relieved of all Housekeeping duties and began working exclusively - as Medical Library Assistant - a position she still has. (See Chapter 26)

In the next chapter, Marla's library job was more in keeping with her fine intellect.

26

Medical Library Assistant
and Christine

INTRODUCTION:

In 1993, Christine was employed as an administrator by the geriatric nursing home where Marla was medical library assistant. The two women soon became acquainted.

Marla was skilled in doing computer work. When time allowed, she did word processing tasks for Christine who was pleased with the results.

In spring 1994, Sheindel the head librarian went on extended sick leave and left undone were several tasks beyond the scope of Marla's usual work. With Christine's executive ability and proximity to the library, she was the logical staff person to begin straightening matters out.

For several months, the library responsibilities fell on Marla's shoulders. As problems arose, Christine worked cooperatively with her.

A head librarian was hired in September 1994 and she became Marla's new supervisor.

Text:
Beginning in 1986, I was officially transferred from Housekeeping to the institution's Medical Library.

I was in frequent conflict with Sheindel, my supervisor, because of my poor social skills and inflexibility. In addition, she hollered at my inability to take library disruptions in stride. She descriminated against disabled people and treated the physically handicapped like dirt.

My initial fear of computerization, she found annoying. Later, when the computer was installed in the library, I became most interested, often reminding Sheindel when it was my turn to use it!

In April 1994, Sheindel became ill and subsequently died in a palliative care hospital.

My happiest period in the library was when I worked alone during late spring and the summer of 1994, because there was no Sheindel mistreating me and I called the shots!

I first got involved with Christine during that period because I needed someone with managerial experience to handle all of Sheindel's unfinished transactions.

In finding Christine approachable and understanding, I told her about my Autism, plus related social problems. Impressed by the quality of my work, she willingly became my workplace advocate; a relationship that lasted almost nine years. (See Chapter 2)

When the new head librarian came on board, Christine provided her with important understanding related to my autism. Also, thanks to Christine, I was allowed to wear casual clothes at work provided they were clean.

To allow for personal errands that might conflict with my mornings in the library, she obtained permission for me to work flexible hours if deemed necessary.

As a support person, Christine helped me cope with emotional crises brought on by such happenings as computer breakdowns, thunder storms and power outages.

Since I worked part-time on a small income, she had me approved for complimentary food tickets, redeemable in the cafeteria.

I was most appreciative when Christine explained my behavior to co-workers, with whom I'd had run-ins, persuading them not to take my hostile demeanor personally.

Her kindness extended beyond the workplace. She made an arrangement with the local ice rink manager, allowing me to skate gratis whenever a group was not scheduled. She would even contact him weekly to find out what days and hours the rink might be available.

In June 2002, Christine broke the news that she was leaving in July for another job. Distraught by the felt loss, there were weeks of insecurity, <u>situational depression</u>* and much sobbing. Anticipating that I'd be having a difficult time without an advocate, she contacted my psychiatrist and social worker to let them know she'd be leaving and suggested they help me adjust to the change.

Since my social worker was employed part-time at <u>CLSC</u>* and told me more than once she had a heavy caseload, those words made it clear that she would not pick up any of the slack caused by my advocate's departure.

A Friday in mid-July was Christine's last day. Without her intervention, I was now at the mercy of mean spirited co-workers who hated my guts, made obvious by their teasing and hostility.

To my dissatisfaction, the head librarian began doing virtually all of the data processing herself - fun computer work that Christine had *shared* with me.

There was nobody to take Christine's place. She had considered two people for the role, but neither wanted it and no staff member volunteered. Without a support person to "run interference," if I get dumped by management for bad behavior, it will come as no surprise.

On account of my severe autism and other neurological problems, finding other employment would be next to impossible. In addition, Quebec law stipulates that a person must be bilingual in French and English to qualify for all but the most menial jobs. Not being fluent in French, I could not be hired. (At the time I began working in this facility, there was no French language requirement, so I've been allowed to continue but *only* in my current position.)

Before leaving, Christine promised to continue being supportive and said I should feel free to telephone her whenever I needed help with difficulties, not job related.

Since she's been gone, it turns out that contacting her for any kind of verbal support or tangible help can be an exercise in futility. She is rarely available due to a demanding executive position, family responsibilities and a busy social life.

Some months prior to Christine's exit, I began noticing a lack of patience when discussing my work-related problems. At times, she seemed cranky and short tempered. But on the whole, over the years, she was a fine person - loyal and supportive. I terribly miss Christine; her departure has left a void in my life.

CONCLUSION:

As a person with severe autism and personality disorders, Marla needs an advocate to deal with inevitable problems that occur in the workplace. With Christine gone and without a supportive replacement, Marla's job has become increasingly stressful.

Christine would provide psychological support when Marla was feeling depressed. When harassed by co-workers, she would intercede on Marla's behalf. Christine would also inform new employees regarding Marla's poor sociality, explaining it was an uncontrollable neurological disorder that should never be taken personally.

Without an advocate, Marla's relationship with several of the co-workers has become increasingly antagonistic, to an extent that her continued employment is uncertain. Frequently getting flack from others in the workplace, Marla becomes terribly distraught.

Depending on her mood, she sometimes worries about getting fired while at other times, due to burnout, she feels a need to bid the job goodbye!

What follows is a disorder that began as a child and continues as an adult. Described in the next chapter are Marla's disobedient, defiant and hostile feelings, especially toward those in authority.

27

Oppositional Defiant Disorder

INTRODUCTION:
ODD oppositional defiant disorder, a childhood dysfunction, is often a precursor to adult PAPD passive aggressive personality disorder.

In Marla's case, the ODD made a seamless transition to PAPD; so that traits of *both disorders coexist* in her adulthood.

Throughout Marla's life, ODD is at least partly responsible for her argumentative nature, frequent loss of temper, general anger, resentment, and irritability. She believes that by expressing ODD, it is a warranted pay-back for life's many injustices.

Text:
Children have at least some ODD traits; it's all a matter of degree. Youngsters tend to resist chores they dislike but do them to please their parents or teachers; perhaps a self-pleasure trait which normal brains are endowed with. I always lacked that emotion; pleasing my parents or the teacher was never my cup of tea.

During twelve years of public schooling and never diagnosed with ODD, I would keep a low profile, slyly ignore the teacher's requests, and "vanish" to a desk in the back row. Day-dreaming much of the time, I did very little work and avoided most class activities. A boy having ODD would tend to act out and be disruptive. Being a girl, that kind of behavior was of no interest to me.

Always a creature living by my own routines, I cannot tolerate submitting to schedules and activities imposed by others. One reason I hated school was my resentment of teachers who would tell us what to do and when to do it. In response, I would shirk class assignments and homework whenever possible - feeling pleasure in whatever I got away with. By using common sense and a process of elimination, I was skillful on tests in answering multiple-choice and true-false questions, so that my grades did not suffer much, despite being inattentive in class and goofing off with homework.

Being sneaky, I got away with petty theft, stealing magnets from classmates in school. And when visiting relatives, I would pilfer antihistamines and other drugs from their bathroom medicine cabinet.

Compared to my childhood and teen years, the oppositional behavior is more extreme as an adult. While growing up I did not suffer the frustrations that have wrecked my adult life. With most everything now going wrong, I have become a rebel - increasingly negative and defiant.

When ODD children get older, they either outgrow the disorder or incorporate it with various kinds of antisocial conduct. The latter has occurred in my case. As a method of retaliation for what I now suffer, the ODD includes a full-blown Passive Aggressive Personality Disorder (PAPD). (See Chapter 33)

Never have I outgrown the childhood ODD practice of much arguing when unable to get my way. Even now, I can still be annoyingly argumentative. In fact, I will, on occasion, deliberately express some of my viewpoints, knowing in advance they can provoke an argument. Then with enjoyment, I'll "shoot down" the other person's point of view with my own strongly held, well thought-out beliefs.

At times when terribly wronged, I spew forth with vulgar language, often out of control. With atrocious weather in the dead of winter, I am prevented from having any exercise. The result is a rotten mood that has my ODD lashing-out at most everyone. Later on, with my head on straight, I'll apologize to those I care about

Mother was to Sherry and Linda a totally *different* parent than the one I experienced; both siblings were normal children while I was a behavioral and societal disaster.

Admittedly, I came into the world with an inborn tendency for ODD. What made it worse was the mismatch between Mother's personality and my ODD temperament. We had a relationship that was doomed from the get-go. She was dead set on forcing me into the mold of a social animal; instead my ODD rebellious tendencies and Mother's fuming opinions - brought out the worst in both of us!

There was no way I would overcome our differences; it was never within my power to become a well-behaved, sociable person - the only kind of daughter she could ever accept.

Dr. Freedman, my Psychiatrist, speculated that even without autism, I'd still have a hard time getting along with people because of my underlying negativity and hostility. He also said that my oppositional personality traits made life far more difficult than it need be. (See Chapter 14)

As assistant librarian, my ODD gets expressed in various ways. On days that I'm especially downcast, I don't brush or comb my hair. I ignore everyone, except the few select people who treat me decently.

A bad-tempered, often uncontrollable personality has worked against me. As it turns out, in a city of millions, I now have but a single support person - my father - but only when he wishes to be available.

If my only severe disorder were autism, I'd theoretically be able to put into practice whatever social skills I've picked up by "osmosis" over the years. Yet, any proper behavior easily gets blocked by *other* disorders. For example, my ODD will cause me to be rude even when I *know* of a more appropriate response.

No one in my life wants to admit that the bulk of my negative behaviors are provoked by adverse, environmental conditions. They put the onus on me, saying I should be more flexible and go with the flow. I could never accept that laid back attitude because fraught with despicable circumstances, I live in a city best described as a dung heap! (See Chapter 9 - Montreal)

CONCLUSION:

By using strict discipline, Mrs. Comm was determined to "cure" all that was *wrong* with her daughter's behavior. The heavy-handed approach not only failed, but served to intensify Marla's ODD traits, already a fact of life inborn and hardwired.

As long as Marla lives in Montreal, her personality will continue on its present course with anger, resentment and vandalism. If she relocates to a decent environment, it is reasonable to believe that she will, in time, display a far less cantankerous persona*.

The next chapter deals with Marla's tendency to oppose people's best suggestions and reject whatever is mandated by authority.

28

Negativity

INTRODUCTION:
Marla admits to a lifelong disposition of negative thinking symptomatic of Autism, and a Co-morbid personality disorder. She is frequently without hope, believing the worst is going to happen. (See Chapters 2 and 21, respectively.)

Due to Montreal's severe climate, economic austerity, dissimilar languages and political unrest, it fails to meet Marla's needs for a satisfactory life. Therefore, her assessment of the city is fraught with negativity. (See Chapter 9)

Each new problem, difficulty or crisis in Marla's awareness easily becomes a topic full of negativity, for those who will listen. (See Chapter 34 - The Quickening)

Because Marla frequently worries and dwells on life's perplexities, her father, co-workers, and acquaintances regard Marla as an extraordinarily negative person. Dr. Freedman believed that her autism was overly biased toward extreme negativism. (See Chapter 14 - Psychiatrist)

Text:
Beginning in the early 1990's and continuing in the new millennium, my life has been on a downward spiral. These days, except for my father, I have nobody in Montreal who cares one whit about me. In addition to the accidental death of my Mother in 2000, Dr. Freedman, my psychiatrist, of over three decades, died of cancer a few years ago. (See Chapter 36 - Mother's Death)

Here are some additional reasons for my negativity:

*The few support people I've had, in years past, have moved and no longer reside in Montreal,

*Because of global climate change the good weather days, for outdoor biking, keep decreasing in number,

*My healthful diet suffers as fresh produce and low-calorie dairy products are either too costly or simply not available,

*World news is nothing but doom and gloom, death and destruction,

*I reject with great disdain materialistic Western society; I abhor what has become a tasteless and vulgar pop-culture,

*Propelling world commerce is extreme greed, motivated by executives with bloated salaries and excessive fringe benefits,

*A preponderance of manufactured goods are crafted with poor design, shoddy workmanship and built-in obsolescence.

All of the above add to my negativity, admittedly a dysfunctional rebel who spurns the planet, who wants to see it destroyed as quickly and painlessly as possible.

With a culture in decline, I've thrown away whatever is left of my life; I have no goals, no ambition and no enthusiasm; my daily interests are limited to simple comforts and basic survival mode; I exert minimal effort in caring for my appearance, neither combing my hair nor otherwise being well-groomed.

Believing that I am chronically negative, whatever the situation, it was so fixed in Dr. Freedman's mind that he never acknowledged my legitimate complaints about Montreal, a city that has failed to meet my needs for <u>tangible</u> <u>support</u>,* exercise, healthful food and daily home care assistance - among other things. (See Chapter 9)

Since I do express occasional pleasure when something good happens in my life, it proves that I am not always a chronic whiner. I would still disagree with my late psychiatrist's over-generalization said more than once: "You'd be unhappy no matter where you live."

For a psychiatrist, I was surprised at his lack of empathy and his own negativity about my points of view. It has always been my belief that with proper food, daily exercise, homecare assistance, emotional support, and living in a warm climate - it would provide a marked improvement from my discontent in Montreal!

In this city there are problems, a can of worms, that warrant negativity and are substantiated by solid evidence that my psychiatrist should have validated: Quebec austerity, inadequate public services, broken roads, frequent crop failure, rotting infrastructure, a vicious climate, and political unrest.

My negativity also has a flip side: I am negative about junk food but positive about low calorie dairy products and fresh vegetables. I am negative in a city of mostly inclement weather but would have positive feelings if living in a small city with a warm, dry climate.

Several years ago, I had legitimate complaints when stuck in an apartment building with vulgar, boisterous neighbors. That I now appreciate living in a condo apartment, among civilized people, is proof that I'm not always negative. And when I *am* negative, there is good reason!

As some people remind me, there are types of Behavior Modification, advocated by mental health professionals that would reduce my negativity. Their use of a "mind game" to make me a less negative person would be a wasted effort. For example, to cure my emotional hatred for Montreal, only a change of locale - the real solution - would relieve the problem. When something is terribly wrong in my life, the deficit must be addressed and not camouflaged by a "brain game." (See Chapter 16)

My father experiences flashes of insight and realizes that much of my negativity stems from Montreal's terrible climate; by not having the financial resources to get me out of here, he is frustrated.

Admittedly, I am more negative than the average person. People, with a less negative attitude, yet faced with adversities, are able to focus on the bright spots in their lives. My personality is such that negative experiences tend to dominate my thinking.

I've learned that society frowns on negativity. It rewards and supports those who are cheerful and rarely complain. Frankly, I am not one of those people, and my negativity is freely expressed to anyone who will listen.

Since I am unable to change Montreal's negatives and I reject behavior modification, my only option is to escape from this deplorable city that feels like a prison. But since I can only work part-time, with an income at the poverty level, I lack the resources to liberate myself.

People don't want to hear my non-smiling litany of complaints, fraught with dissatisfaction and resentment. It is one reason, I get no more than an occasional crumb of support, from anyone I know.

Between my negativity and lacking a sense of Humor, I am terribly unpopular. (See Chapter 24)

Scientists are beginning to think that specific modules of the brain control positive and negative thinking. If true, my negative module is dominant.

Based on genetics and like many personality traits, negativity is a characteristic that can be inherited. In fact, my maternal Aunt Hilda's personality abounds with as much negativity as mine; I suspect a genetic link.

Mine is a history of family mistreatment, partly responsible for the extent of my negativity trait, years of parental verbal abuse, their threats and rejection. I've read that countless people who become child abusers were themselves mistreated when growing up. I believe that my reactive behavior is, in part, an unconscious payback for what I endured growing up. When angered by someone, I am quick to retaliate; it can be with foul language, name-calling, and scathing, criticisms.

One of my disorders is a Passive-Aggressive Personality, often referred to as a "negativistic personality disorder," in which the trait of negativity is paramount." (See Chapter 33) I cannot tolerate poor service in a retail store, and not grumble foul remarks within earshot of customers and the employee. Then, to get additional respite, I must later vent the aggravating incident to anyone receptive, since it does reduce any "leftover sting," from the store clerk incident.

Dr. Freedman told me that if I were a less negative person, I would realize that my life is really not so bad, especially since becoming assistant medical librarian, the best job I've ever had.

Though the job is an improvement, it does have many flaws: no advocate to assist with my people problems; an increasingly heavy workload; no increase in salary despite years of inflation and higher taxes - just a few of the job's many negatives. (See Chapter 26 - Medical Library Assistant)

When someone assaults me with the word "hopefully," it conflicts with my negative state of mind and I tell them it's an expression that should be obliterated from the dictionary.

The crux of my thinking now goes beyond atheism; it now encompasses a nihilistic philosophy which rejects all of society's established institutions, not just religion. I reject everything from medical science to pop culture to social values that include marriage, family, and babies. When in a negative mood, I don't hesitate to express my unconventional opinions; I could not care less what other people think of me!

CONCLUSION:
Marla's negativity is severe and parallels extraordinary unhappiness. Since so much of it is based on living in the wrong environment, the only alternative for a better life is moving out of Montreal to a small city with a temperate climate. I believe that if she lived under better conditions, her demeanor would reflect far less of the negativity that is now so much a part of her personality.

As made clear in the next chapter, Marla stands firm on her fixed principles, purposes, and viewpoints.

29

Inflexibility and Candor

INTRODUCTION:
Marla possesses considerable self-knowledge as to many of the motivational forces behind her thoughts and behavior. She also expresses herself with remarkable candor. None of these positive traits result in change for what is a strikingly, inflexible lifestyle.

Text:
Admittedly, I have a willingness to discuss, with much candor, my life's story through e-mail correspondence and in person. I may be looking for solutions to my worries and dilemmas. Also, venting the problems, at least momentarily, relieves some of the stress.

Dr. Freedman, my late psychiatrist, once remarked that my degree of openness is unusual for an adult with high functioning autism. He considered it a social error to be inappropriately candid with one's personal matters and private feelings, especially with people I hardly know.

Borderline Personality traits lead to emotional emptiness; and with my need to communicate, it does motivate considerable candor. Also, when discussing my hardships, there is the possibility someone may know where I can get help, even offering it themselves, i.e. psychological* and/or tangible support*. If they offer nothing in that regard, I may at least gain their Interpersonal Validation; even that much feels good! (See Chapter s 32 and 15, respectively.)

Others may think of me as a lazy, whining person who refuses to help herself; surely an intelligent individual should be able to solve her own problems! They don't want to hear my troubles unless accompanied by flexibility and a willingness to experiment with some of the solutions they offer.

Unwittingly, they are misled by my good intelligence and candid explanations; those qualities can mask the extent of my dysfunctional worries, problems and inflexibility.

People get tired of listening to my constant complaints about living in overcrowded Montreal with its anti-Anglo bias and a cold fish Francophone majority. They would be more understanding if I showed them specific steps I was taking to relocate; problem is I lack the financial resources to do it.

When crying the "poverty blues," I notice a lack of interest in my plight. People don't want to hear about it unless there is tangible evidence that I'm trying to solve the problem by working more hours or taking courses leading to a higher paying job. They forget I am barely surviving and I suffer what is best described as a "mental burnout." They fail to realize that I lack the cognitive and emotional energy to work on changes that might improve my quality of life. (See Chapter 23 - Chronic Nervous Fatigue)

CONCLUSION:
We live in a society that champions the principle of solving whatever problems in our life need fixing. Mental health professionals are reluctant to accept the idea that a highly intelligent person's neurology can be so inflexible that meaningful self-improvement is not possible.

As a person with multiple <u>neuro-disorders</u>* and worn out from chronic nervous system fatigue, Marla's day-to-day living has become so tenuous that holding on to her *familiar* routines is the only way of maintaining a degree of stability.

While her candor can encourage good advice from others, it does not, in any way, lead to a more productive lifestyle. Inflexibility and brain fatigue disallow any improvement in her dysfunctional circumstances.

Locating out of Montreal is the only lifestyle change of interest to Marla; the only opportunity to turn her life around.

On a more positive note, the next chapter is about Marla earning a university degree in mathematics.

30

College Degree

INTRODUCTION:
Throughout grade school and high school, Marla excelled in math. In 1982, she entered Concordia College, in Montreal, and began working toward a BS degree with honors in math.

To earn a living, she continued working part-time, and could maintain her studies by taking no more than two or three subjects each semester.

Text:
Because of early registration, I was able to sign up for the coming semester weeks or months in advance. I would then purchase the required texts and - on my own - get started learning the new material. Once the term officially started, I was able to use the class lectures mainly for review.

This method worked well, except for one math professor who enjoyed interacting with the class. He would get noticeably upset when a student was not intent on his lecture. Already knowing the material, I must have seemed disinterested because he reprimanded me for not paying attention. However, since I aced the final exam, apparently class demeanor had no effect on my final grade.

One of the course requirements was an introduction to computer science. In those days, I had no enthusiasm for computers nor did I think they had much value, other than being used for sundry business applications. Much of the course work dealt with learning programming skills and using computer software.

Despite the complexities of programming and having no great interest in computers, I managed to finish the course with a high mark.

There was also a required biology course. Except for topics related to the study of humans, I had no interest in the other subject matter and did not exert myself in topics dealing with plants and animals. For the final exam I lucked-out because we could choose any five out of ten questions, and I was able to *avoid* all of the ones dealing with non-human topics

Ironically, for all the time, effort and money spent on the university courses, the only ones ever put to practical use were the computer electives. It all happened when my workplace began using computers in 1992, and I became interested in mastering the software. Because the computers were used for realistic applications of record keeping and data processing, affecting the nursing home, I found the work challenging and worthwhile.

Although not part of my assistant-librarian job description, I taught myself how to use word processing and other software. In becoming somewhat of an authority, I enthusiastically helped nurses and office workers solve computer problems in their departments.

I always had a knack for learning the linear logic of high school and college math and since computers employ a similar logic, it explains my ability to teach myself and others various software skills.

Certain facts always stick in my mind, not due to an exceptional memory or intelligence but because they have a logic - a kind of reasoning - that my brain can understand. What might seem like unusual recall ability, to another person, is for me a linear connection between one set of facts and another. Once I learn the "formula," I can easily apply it to other situations; call it an ability to detect a similarity, wherever one exists.

My stress with university life involved more than mastering the course work; other demands could also be troubling. For example, a final exam time and date rarely coincided with the regular afternoon class schedule; I often got stuck with taking the end term exam at night and causing two problems: Interference with my inflexible evening routine and diminished thinking ability due to the late hour.

I was teased by classmates, from the way I reacted to some of the class procedures, becoming fearful whenever graded papers were being returned. For me, anything less than 100% was unacceptable and equivalent to a failing mark!

I recall a severe emotional reaction when the professor told us that an exam scheduled for the following afternoon had been re-scheduled for an evening hour. In a state of anxiety, I frantically waved my hand to get his attention and contrived a health problem: due to fatigue, I could not think clearly at night and begged him to let me take the exam during the daytime. He looked puzzled, while the students began laughing - no doubt convinced I was off my rocker!

To my relief, he granted my wish and the next afternoon I sat in a cold room next to the ice hockey rink where I nearly froze to death. But the physical discomfort was lots better than having to miss my all important evening routine. (See Kitchen Chores, page 78)

I'm well aware of lacking cognitive abilities that are needed to fully understand all facets of a subject. That my intellectual progress is limited, even in math, was made painfully clear.

After earning a BS math degree with high marks, I enrolled in a master's program. Early in the first semester, I realized that the theoretical math being taught was beyond my comprehension; my forte of linear logic was of no use to me at the graduate level; the complexities of *lateral* thinking were beyond my understanding. After much stress but with a sense of relief, I dropped out of the program later in the semester.

In retrospect, I wonder how deep an interest in math I really had, because I was never so engrossed that I forgot about food or exercise. Also, I never had a desire to attend special math seminars or embark on a project of my own.

As to a profession in math and knowing it was high-time to start thinking about a career, I found myself at a dead end. I had absolutely no interest in applying the math to anything practical; it never went any further than learning what each course had to offer and ace every exam.

As for becoming a high school math teacher - but unable to hide my autism - I'd be humiliated standing in front of 30 or 40 students, having a "field day," whispering and giggling about my weird idiosyncrasies. (See Chapter 2 - Autism)

CONCLUSION:

Marla's strong liking for math has an explanation. Due to its absoluteness, it is a unique scientific discipline because either a theorem is true or is false. Once proven and known to be flawless, its truth is final. This unique feature was especially appealing to Marla, and helped earn a college degree in math.

Marla has no interest in a teaching career nor could her central nervous system withstand the stress of one. Except for some occasional private tutoring no practical use was ever made of her unusual math ability.

She continues working part-time, as an assistant medical librarian in a geriatric-care nursing home. Her workplace responsibilities include computer data processing which she finds appealing and executes with considerable skill.

The next chapter discusses the anomaly of Marla's high intelligence but poor motivation.

31

Intellect and Low Motivation

INTRODUCTION:
Marla's high functioning IQ intelligence quotient works for and against her. In a positive sense, she earned a bachelor's degree in mathematics and to her credit she is well-versed in a wide range of medical, neurological, psychiatric, and computer topics.

However, it angers Marla that people expect more from her in terms of career accomplishments than her neurological disorders can withstand or deliver.

Text:
My dysfunctional neurological disorders are not lessened in severity by having a respectable IQ. Often surprised by my self-defeating attitudes and behavior, people do not understand that my IQ does not help matters. (See Chapter 33 - Passive-Aggressive Personality Disorder.)

Desirous of learning more about my neurological disorders, I have done extensive psychiatric reading, in *bits* and *pieces*, over the years. Unfortunately, any resulting insight has neither modified the suffering nor lessened my dysfunctional, acting-out behavior.

Despite a good IQ, I do have intellectual weaknesses. For instance, with ADD/H, I cannot do sustained reading for more than 10 or 15 minutes. Also, with articles of interest in medical journals and the Internet, I mainly research my own neurological disorders - ways they affect me narrowly and in <u>synergy</u>*. Obviously, I'm not a person with a *wide ranging* thirst for knowledge. (See Chapter 5 - Attention Deficit Disorder/Hyperactivity)

For me, language ability is a mixed bag; I have no skill, at all, in the social aspects of language called pragmatics. There is also difficulty understanding non-literal language such as metaphors, sayings and jokes; a tendency to take whatever people say, literally - symptomatic of Autism. (See Chapter 2)

Due to autism, when orally expressing myself, what I say is often misunderstood; I have difficulty organizing my thoughts into an orderly and functional manner of stating something.

Autism also affects my intellect; whether at home or at work, my imagination and creativity are poor; they are unable to cope with many of the daily problems that ordinarily arise.

Because of autistic inflexibility, I am strictly a creature of habit and *fixed routines*; adapting myself to any substitute circumstance is mostly impossible.

Also, my brain hardwiring of poor hand-eye coordination, precludes any interest, or ability, in the fine arts, such as playing an instrument, painting a picture or doing sculpture. (See Chapter 17 - Dyspraxia).

As a teenager, I began taking piano lessons. At that time, I may have had a modicum of musical ability because at the piano and despite my clumsy hands, I could play simple Jewish dances by ear. Because of dyspraxia and my failure in learning to read notes, the instructor lost patience; and unable to tolerate his criticism, I quit taking lessons.

On an IQ test, the subtests that might give me trouble are tasks of arranging sets of people-pictures in proper sequence; they are designed to evaluate a person's sociality, empathy and imagination. Autistic people, typically lacking in those skills, do poorly on that part of the exam; I am no exception.

A function of *visual-spatial ability*, not tested by the standard IQ test, is one's knack of organizing objects in space, nor is *practical intelligence* covered. I am terribly lacking in both abilities; they are Co-morbid and have me dysfunctional in keeping house and being organized when working in the library. In both places the clutter abounds. Periodically, the supervisor needs to help me straighten out the hodgepodge in my work area. (See Chapter 21)

I can neither remember where I put things nor can I organize objects in drawers, closets, and cabinets. My condo apartment is a mass of papers, clothing and sundry objects scattered all over. (See Chapter 20 - Executive Function Disorder)

Besides organizing ability, visual-spatial skills involve the brain's ability to accurately interpret information received from the eyes, such as the distance between oneself and that of objects or people in the vicinity; and whether individuals are stationary or moving. I am especially weak in this skill. When skating or biking, I get very nervous when others get too close, and fear they will crash into me. As a precaution, I slow down and let them go ahead of me.

I also have problems dealing with uncertainty when something is neither black nor white. When alternatives are possible, there is my dilemma of choosing the best one and I have a tendency to mull over the best outcome, far too long.

I do not trust current events in the news media; it is difficult to distinguish factual truth from media exaggeration. I, therefore, rely on my father to clear up any uncertainties.

My intellect is of zilch help during an emergency. A power failure will throw me into a panic; unable to make use of what I cognitively know - namely that the power will be restored. It is believed that an emotional meltdown is the result of *neuron disconnections,* affecting proper communication between the brain's emotional and cognitive areas. (See Chapter 7 - Anxiety and Meltdowns)

People criticize me for not accomplishing more with my life. I admit to not making sufficient use of my intelligence; problem is, I possess few of the traits commonly found in people who have an intellectual predisposition. Unlike them, I do not crave challenges but prefer routine work. I am neither creative nor do I have a thirst for knowledge. I cannot spend hours immersed in books or laboratory work. Bright people discuss all manner of intellectual topics; not having their mentality, I could not withstand the boredom.

Life in Montreal is mentally killing me. I have little or no desire to succeed at anything except pranks and Passive-Aggressive vandalism, used to vent my anger. (See Chapter 33)

While I cannot make full use of basic intelligence, it helps prevent emotional flare-ups from verbally or physically getting out of control. Despite extreme anger toward someone and while I may fantasize violence, I've always had enough sense to refrain from it.

My brain is alert when spoiling or damaging supermarket junk food and great care is exercised in not getting caught. I also limit the dollar amount of each trashed item. Then if I should get discovered, I could cough up enough money to pay for the damage and avoid any police involvement.

When growing up, I was mainstreamed in a mediocre public school system and received no special help, not even an acknowledgement of my autism. However, a crafty intellect allowed me to "beat the system" and achieve *passing* grades, even in the *people subjects* that left me clueless - especially in literature and history! Multiple choice and true-false tests were my artful talents; a modus operandi that saved the day and forestalled some of the parental anger when seeing uneven grades on my report card.

A "third degree" at the supper table was non-stop questioning about the school day and my assigned homework. If a teacher contacted my parents regarding mediocre performance in the people subjects, I got a tongue-lashing! They expected me to do well in *every* subject. Lacking sophistication, they did not understand that my uneven ability was caused by autism and other disorders. For them a passing grade was not enough; they wanted straight A in everything!

Being in denial* of my autism and a false belief that I had innate academic ability, I was a misfit being sent to a regular public school. All the while, I needed special education in a private school which may have given me individualized instruction for my unequal subject aptitude. (See Chapter 1 - Childhood and Teen Years)

However, in my favor is having a good long-term memory. I can recall countless incidents, occurring over the years, which provided insight into my neuro-disorders* and atypical behaviors. A receptive memory allows the bits-and-pieces of learning to cumulatively increase my knowledge base. With most everyone, the important events occurring in their life become one extended blur. In contrast, I am able to remember specific dates, people incidents and important happenings - especially those connected with emotional trauma.

I admit to have a lifelong fascination with numbers. The IQ subtests of arithmetical reasoning, verbal ability and general comprehension were sub-tests in which I did well. In contrast, subjects dealing with people and sociality gave me big trouble. (See Chapter 2 - Autism)

I get annoyed by having a reputation of good intellect. Being bright often works against me; it misleads people into overestimating abilities that are "road blocked" by multiple brain disorders. I recall that upon earning my BS degree, I tutored some staff nurses in advanced math; word soon spread that I was some kind of a genius!

The way most people see it, a BS degree in math does not reconcile with Medical Library Assistant; surely someone with my intelligence could be doing a great deal more! When explaining my disabilities, I often get a stock response to the effect: "You can overcome any handicap; it is purely a matter of willpower and determination!" (See Chapter 26)

Their expectations have no limit: They talk about learning to be flexible, cultivating new interests, making friends, getting a PhD, and so on. As it is, now, with all of my Invisible disabilities, I can barely get through the day. As long as bare, day-to-day survival is the name of the game, my state of mind will not tolerate the slightest amount of personal improvement. People find it hard to believe that an intelligent person can also have <u>hardwired</u>* personality dysfunctions, preventing a normal life. (See Chapter 21)

Nor do people understand brain functions: They think of the brain as a single unit; so that if I'm skilled in math, I can then do most anything. They do not realize there are countless areas of the brain, each creating an arrangement of abilities and deficits - composites of strengths and weaknesses.

Being overwrought by 9/11, I told my father we might all die or be condemned to lives of suffering if terrorism escalated into a third world war. He angrily barked at me, "Marla, I thought you were smart!" I told him to forget about math achievements and realize that I am not "smart" in everything and that coping with hard times is not my strong suit. And a good IQ does not help me contend with the terrorism and stressors of the new millennium. (See Chapter 34 - The Quickening)

Besides people expecting too much out of me, a good IQ can be a millennium disadvantage. I have far more understanding than most people have of the countless Quickening issues now threatening world stability. Lucky are those who have no qualms and can put life's menaces on the backburner.

Nowadays, if anyone says they've heard I'm brilliant, they get a stock response: "I do have above average math ability but in other respects I'm really quite ordinary."

With dysfunctional neurological baggage and trying to live in the mainstream of an abrasive, overcrowded city - the separate entity of my intellect does not serve me well. (See Chapter 9 - Montreal)

Despite having a good IQ, I am without the "practical intelligence" needed for day-to-day survival in the mainstream. My struggle to survive, in the midst of adverse and despicable conditions is tenuous at best; an existence of living on the edge! (See Chapter 35 - Suicidal Thoughts)

(Practical intelligence is an ability to solve life's everyday problems; to find the best fit between oneself and demands of the environment. It is a concept developed by Dr. Robert Sternberg*.)

CONCLUSION:
It is reasonable to hypothesize that Marla suffered considerable brain damage during gestation, affecting certain parts of the brain, while leaving some intellectual areas mostly unscathed.

Because of a multiplicity of neurological disorders, including autism and attention deficit disorder, the practical functioning of Marla's high intelligence has been seriously compromised. People have yet to learn that neurological functions are served by various areas of the brain, so that high intelligence in one area does not imply similar levels of ability in other brain areas.

If one defines intelligence, based on what the standard IQ test measures, Marla's overall score is well above average.

The next chapter is characterized by Marla's personality traits of black-and-white thinking, mood swings, faulty emotional reasoning and abnormal social functioning.

32

Borderline Personality Disorder

INTRODUCTION:

Marla's BPD borderline personality disorder is an ongoing pattern of instability. She will experience bouts of anger, situational depression and anxiety that may last only hours or typically not more than a day. BPD negatively affects her interpersonal relations, self-image and emotions. She believes BPD is caused by a biological predisposition, made more acute by a childhood fraught with verbal abuse and rejection.

Dr. Freedman, Marla's psychiatrist, diagnosed her as having borderline personality *traits* rather than a full-blown BPD condition. He was reluctant to use the BPD label, not sure which of the traits were primarily due to BPD, Autism or Tourette Syndrome. For example, her anger outbursts may be caused by any of the three disorders acting individually or in synergy. (See Chapters 2 and 6, respectively.)

BPD serves to reinforce Marla's Passive-Aggressive Personality Disorder. By an overlapping of both disorders, they can act in synergy to intensify her PAPD. (See Chapter 33)

Marla's BPD traits include the following:
*BPD overlapping of passive aggressive personality disorder,
*Fear of abandonment,
*Over-sensitivity to environmental circumstances,
*Low self-esteem,
*Sudden shifts in her evaluation of people, called splitting.
*Unstable self-image,
*Occasional feeling of non-existence,
*Recurrent suicidal thoughts,
Anxiety, depression, stress (mostly situational),
*Periods of anger, panic and despair,
Extreme reactions to NT people, in synergy* with autism,
*Chronic feelings of emptiness and emotional insecurity,
*Difficulty controlling anger and verbal outbursts, in synergy
   with Tourette and autism,
*Substance abuse for escape into Oblivion (See Chapter 12),
*BPD Self-Abuse in synergy with Dyspraxia and Sensory-
   Integration (See Chapters 11,17 and 18, respectively).

Text:
Low self-esteem and being an *outcast* best describes my childhood
inside and outside the home. I lacked the physical ability and social
skills to join in peer games. There were never any friendships with
co-equals nor did I ever want one.

I could, however, relate to my brain impaired cousin, Bryna, who
during gestation suffered brain damage, believed caused by her
mother's alcohol addiction. There were also a few mentally retarded
neighborhood kids who sometimes played with me. Because of their
brain dysfunctions, the games proved less than satisfactory, but at
least they didn't make fun of me as did normal kids.

By resisting the social values treasured by my parents; I was made
to feel worthless. Stylish clothes, a circle of friends and people events
were values I vehemently rejected; a renunciation based on social
negativity, the consequence of autism, a disorder which neither par-

ent believed I had. However, they were puzzled by its inconsistency; though my behavior was outrageous and unacceptable, it was in marked contrast with good intelligence. (See Chapter 31-Intellect)

I believe my low self-esteem is a BPD combination of genetic influences, life's hard knocks, personal failures and verbal abuse dished out by my parents - hypercritical of most everything I said and did. (See Chapter 1 - Childhood and Teen Years)

A known risk factor causing BPD are parents who habitually invalidate what their child says, certainly the case with my mother. She would believe another person's account of a misbehavior and disbelieve my version of what *actually* happened. In her estimation, I was always "guilty" until proven "innocent;" it was treatment that interfered with my feelings of self-worth developing.

At age 19, I moved-out of the family home. Lacking both self-esteem and Executive Function skills, I was ill-equipped for life in the mainstream of an abrasive, metropolitan city. (See Chapter 20)

My dysfunctional condition has never improved, with life impossibly difficult to handle; I have neither pride in myself nor the ability to function with adequate independence.

By having an unsatisfactory life, I suffer from frequent mood disorders characterized by worry, stress, irritability, situational depression and bouts of anxiety.

Even on days of suitable biking weather, my preferred exercise, I can still retain hostile and irritable moods related to: financial problems, stressors* at work, confrontations with co-workers, and lack of support from the few people I depend on. During inclement weather and forced to remain at home, I am denied Exercise. A state of bad temperament then prevails: sadness, tears, anger, low self-worth and suicidal thoughts. (See Chapter 12)

My BPD instability occurs in relationships with people I deal with in daily life - co-workers, service providers, and anyone I depend on for support. My mood and behavior will reflect the amount of cooperation forthcoming and can easily flip-flop from high regard to deep hatred. This emotional and behavioral toggling, back-and-forth, is a trait symptomatic of BPD, acting in synergy with autism.

Admittedly, my common sense gets beaten down by intense emotion. For example, I have difficulty coming to grips with the idea that the same individual, depending on their mood, will at times display contradictory selves; I can then have a totally opposite change of feeling toward the person which in BPD parlance is called "splitting."

When I was a nurse's aide, years ago, there were incidents of *splitting* that occurred with my supervisor. I found her caring and friendly if she let me have my own way; yet I would feel a deep hatred, for her, whenever she strictly enforced the rules.

With any patient assigned to me, I always insisted on working alone. One reason I could not tolerate a co-worker was due to my BPD emotion of *non-existence* - the empty feeling of getting "absorbed" into another person who'd be active and in tandem with me.

With poor hand-eye coordination, yet trying to do Kitchen Chores, the result is anger, despair and self-abuse. I have chipped my teeth biting counter tops, smashed cabinets, and in recent years substituted self-mutilation - biting my arms to vent frustration and rage - while not damaging the kitchen. (See Chapter 11)

As for the biting, this BPD self-abuse is also a cry for help; perhaps a caring individual will notice my arms with blood and sores; proof positive that I need help; perhaps willing to assist me in the kitchen or may know of an individual or a charitable agency able to help me.

I feel worthless, lacking the financial resources that would get me out of a city slowly destroying me. When in a hopeless BPD mood, with no outs, I begin contemplating the Swiss option. (Under Swiss law, assisted suicide is legal.) My wretched existence in Montreal has been snuffing out any desire to live; just getting out of bed in the morning and facing a new day, requires a Herculean effort! (See Chapter 9)

A chronic feeling of emptiness is one of my BPD traits. I am fed up with co-workers and others suggesting activities that would supposedly give me fulfillment: reading novels, taking courses, watching movies, or doing volunteer work. By now, they should know me well-enough to realize those "time-wasters" would produce nothing but more stress and increased boredom.

When comparing myself to people whose brains appear to function normally, my low self-esteem is worsened by feelings of inferiority.

Neighbors have scorned me because of my outrageous screaming during a power outage. In places I've lived, people have referred to me as a "mental case." (See Chapter 7 - Emotional Meltdown)

Both parents have added to my unstable self-image; they've considered me nothing but trouble - smashing kitchens, getting my bike stolen, breaking a key in the front door lock, and some other short-comings. They could never find positives in my life to offset the negatives. The feeling of being a "rotten apple" was escalated and fed by two of Mother's pet expressions: "With you Marla, it's always something." and "You're a person only a mother could love!"

In an e-mail written to a support person, I told him: "My supervisor has an atrocious handwriting but when at a loss to decipher her scribbling, she is very patient with me." The pen-pal responded: "While this was a small incident, it illustrates an important truth; namely, if your boss had illegible handwriting, she is lucky that *you* were patient with *her* and not vice versa; you were deserving of an apology for something that was unreadable. I mention this to illustrate the extent to which your ego has been crushed - blaming yourself, when someone else is clearly at fault." I told him that his insight was right on target!

In search of understanding and living in a city beyond my ability to cope, I verbally complain about temporary issues. However, intermittent difficulties are not so much at issue; rather it is the frequency, tenacity and compulsivity of my despair that are so problematic and symptomatic of BPD.

I have sought to compensate for low self-esteem by urging others to agree with my viewpoints, related to Montreal and even The Quickening. Because individual opinions can be strikingly diverse, I get limited Interpersonal Validation, on most issues. (See Chapters 34 and 15, respectively)

Since I'm a chronic complainer, co-workers and others mistakenly consider me a person who can never be satisfied. I have tried to convince them, otherwise. While never becoming the world's happiest person, I could at least achieve a more fulfilled life, in a small city with a good climate.

In the meantime, while I'm suffering in Montreal and have to deal with the daily problems, I need ongoing psychological* and occasional tangible support*. Each evening, I need to speak on the phone with my father to unburden various happenings of the day. If the conversation goes well, I feel more relaxed and better able to get a decent night's sleep. Unfortunately, he doesn't always call.

There are BPD feelings of being worthless, lost and abandoned when my father, a support person I depend on, travels out of the city or is otherwise unavailable. Though I rely on him for tangible support and the evening phone call; he refuses to arrange for backup support while he's gone, despite knowing full well, I must have someone to take his place - an urgent need that borders on desperation!

CONCLUSION:

Marla's feelings and emotional needs were oppressed by a family spewing forth their verbal abuse. By squelching Marla's very essence, it prevented her from developing a normal sense of self.

The verbal abuse included a denial of her autism, frequent criticism, insults, insinuations, and accusations - all of it causing a lifelong undoing of Marla's self-image.

In Marla's preference to remain aloof from others, rarely does anyone volunteer to befriend her.

Because of BPD splitting, she will alternately idealize and devalue the same person.

Growing up and also during the adult years, there has never been anyone with whom Marla could identify; no role model throughout her entire life - always a *loner* in every sense of the word.

It is extremely difficult or impossible for a psychiatrist to help eliminate or modify the BPD traits of an adult. What appears to a mental health specialist as a serious personality dysfunction is often perceived as logical and rational by individuals like Marla and others with the disorder.

A cardinal feature of Marla's BPD is an emotional insecurity that pervades her life. She is highly sensitive to frustrations and unmet expectations; they activate rage, despondency, situational depression, emotional meltdowns, self-abuse and suicidal thoughts.

For Marla's BPD, the only possible change for the better would be an improved environment that would minimize some of the stressors that trigger her dysfunctional feelings and behaviors.

The next chapter describes another personality disorder, pertaining to behavior, in which Marla's feelings of aggression are acted out.

33

Passive-Aggressive Personality Disorder

INTRODUCTION:
Marla's PAPD passive-aggressive personality disorder is primarily an adult disorder, but with childhood roots emanating from Oppositional Defiant Disorder. (See Chapter 27)

Passive-aggression is considered "passive" because it is indirect and does not involve a direct confrontation; Marla's vandalism, done surreptitiously, falls into that category.

She will also express some of her aggression, rebellion and hostility in PAPD ways, other then vandalism.

Text:
During my mid-teens, I went through a rebellious PAPD phase of deliberately walking into the house with mud on my shoes. The more Mother hollered, the more I was motivated to do, on purpose, what seemed like absent-minded behavior.

To spite my parents, I also went through a stage of bathing infrequently. While a certain amount of PAPD rebellious behavior is normal during the teen years, mine was extreme! Also, instances of petty theft were not unusual.

Gravol pills relieve the nausea and vomiting that accompanies the onset of flu. As a teenager, I would steal Gravol from drugstores and relatives' medicine cabinets. It was at a time during a stomach flu epidemic and I was deathly afraid of catching it. My phobic fear of vomiting drove me to steal the pills, so I'd always be sure of having an ample supply. (See Chapter 22 - Vomiting Phobia)

The following are a cross-section of PAPD during various stages of my life:

As a kid, there were pranks I knew would not be blamed on me, such as: throwing away my classmate's lunch during a field trip and the pleasure of seeing her get upset.

Father's beverage bar was located near my bedroom in the basement; I recall sneaking his alcoholic drinks to calm my nerves.

In my late teens and early twenties, I shoplifted food from grocery stores and was caught a few times stealing diet candies and low-fat cottage cheese. Since I offered to pay for the items, my parents were never informed.

When I was alone in the Laundromat, with a machine in motion, a favorite caper was tossing a bunch of Kleenex into someone's wash; thereby creating a yucky mess that gave me pleasure.

In the late seventies, when I worked as a nurse's aide, I noticed that the night-staff kitchen was sometimes left unlocked. I would then sneak in and help myself to leftovers which I doggy-bagged and later took home.

One morning, I saw that the key had been left in the night-kitchen lock. Since no one was around, I put the key in my purse and hurried to have a duplicate made at a nearby locksmith. Then, returning to the kitchen, I placed the original key back in the lock. Subsequently, every morning before work and by using my key, I had free access to the night kitchen. It allowed me to "liberate" some of the leftovers, stash them in my purse to enjoy later when I got home.

I once played a trick on my library boss by rigging her PC word processor, so that whatever key she pressed, it typed the letter "a." She was naturally upset! A few days later, I fixed the PC before she came to work, and never was she able to figure out what caused the keyboard to suddenly function normally!

I had an obsession of liking the vintage, red phone booths on the streets of Montreal. To my dismay, in 1992, I noticed the red booths were being replaced with ordinary ones, of no interest to me. I was determined to snap a few pictures of the few remaining red ones, before they all disappeared. I also needed to take a few photographs of the kitchen I had smashed-up, in a condo apartment, to show my psychiatrist. (See Chapter 11 - Kitchen Chores)

My plan was to "borrow" my father's camera and then return it without him being any the wiser. I didn't want to ask permission because he'd either say "no" or hound me with questions as to why I needed to use it. Having a key to the house, I went there one day when my parents weren't at home and removed the camera from a ledge in the living room. I then purchased film and during the week I took several pictures, as planned.

I had no opportunity to return the camera before they realized it was missing from the ledge. Being the only other person with access to the house, they questioned me continually, but I denied knowing anything about it.

One afternoon, I slipped into the house when nobody was at home and put the camera into one of their suitcases in the basement. I was hopeful they'd assume that after returning from a trip, it had been left in the luggage. By not checking the basement luggage, their third degree became angrier with each passing day!

Finally, in deciding to go through the luggage, they located the camera in a decrepit suitcase that had not been used in years. As the only other person with access to the house, I had to have done it and they berated me harshly; and then to make matters worse, I lied about it!

They even telephoned my psychiatrist to get his advice on how best to handle the deception. Since all I did was borrow the camera, he minimized the problem and advised them to overlook it. Instead, his counsel was ignored and their angry words continued, non-stop, for a couple of weeks!

These days, I can hardly go into a supermarket without feeling an urge to trash some junk food. It provides an *emotional release* that allows me to continue functioning, despite an ever worsening food situation; since affordable low-calorie food items are mostly not available, it infuriates me that junk food versions are plentiful and often on special. Vandalizing "pig food" will not mean lower prices for the products I need, or changes in store policy, however, it does release my pent-up anger. (See Chapter 10 - Food Shopping)

Though not often my experience, but when a shopping trip is successful, I simply pay for the items and leave the store without inflicting any damage

My vandalism is also connected with poverty. If I had ample money and were able to afford healthful products regardless of cost, there'd be no urge to damage any junk food.

As for vandalism, some of my capers are squashing loaves of bread, digging my nails into bananas (high in calories), and hiding cartons of fattening ice cream in warm places. A favorite trick is unscrewing bottle caps of cranberry-cocktail juice, mostly sugar water.

I minimize the chances of getting caught and since Montreal supermarkets are usually overcrowded, I'm not likely to be noticed.

While in the process of destroying the worthless food, there is a sense of satisfaction. Even if the store manager doesn't know that my vandalism is a protest, I feel pleasure knowing he'll be annoyed, by having to dispose of the damaged items.

Vandalizing also serves the broader purpose of getting even with, what I consider to be, an uncaring and unjust society. When feeling wronged, the literature discusses individuals having passive-aggressive behavior and oppositional traits, with a compulsion to get even with the "system." I precisely fit that description! If I had only one day to live, my final mission on earth would be to ransack a major supermarket and destroy every bit of junk food.

If the worth of my supermarket vandalism never exceeds a few dollars, the worst likely scenario is having to pay for the items - an experience that happened a few years ago. A store flyer advertised Jello at a reasonable price and I went there, expecting to buy some. With a dozen boxes of sugarless Jello in my shopping basket and having stood 15 minutes on the checkout line, I was told that only regular Jello was included in the sale, not the sugarless variety.

Infuriated, I grabbed a box of the sugar Jello, on special, and began squishing the box with uncontrollable rage! An employee saw this and as I was leaving the store, he grabbed my arm. I tried biting his forearm but only managed to catch his sleeve between my teeth!

Told to either pay for the ruined Jello or face arrest, I willingly paid the 33 cents and bailed myself out of a tight situation. As my final provocation, I held up the damaged box, screamed at my captor plus everyone in earshot: "I have no use for this worthless junk loaded with sugar, but I know of someone's mutt who will devour every bit of it."

I also engage in a one person rebellion against the pervasive junk food served in my workplace cafeteria. I use my gratis tickets to obtain servings of mashed potatoes, canned corn and other worthless starch. When no one is looking, I dump the pig food into a trash can; since "garbage" belongs in a garbage can that's where it goes!

The argumentativeness and rudeness I exhibit, in various situations, are aspects of my PAPD disposition. It includes: over-complaining when things go wrong, grumbling when forced to be compliant and a general pattern of negativistic, ill-tempered behavior.

At work, I don't have major problems with defiance but do feel an inner rebellion when forced to stop what I'm doing, in response to my supervisor's sudden rush order, or listen to her explain something when I'm in the midst of essential work, requiring my full attention.

All my life, I've been mentally at war with authorities such as schoolteachers, policemen and bosses. If a person in authority is within my sight or hearing, I find it stressful. If I'm forced to obey rules laid down by someone else, I might as well be in prison!

Symptomatic of PAPD is being envious of others, begrudging their good fortune when they are successful or lucky. One reason I developed a dysfunctional relationship with my sister Sherry was envy, pure and simple! I thought of her as being *perfect* in so many ways - enjoying life's material and social pleasures, in ways foreign to my HFA* personality - human advantages I could never achieve.

Getting back to the supermarket, when shopping and waiting on the check-out line, crawling at a snail's pace, I respond by muttering words pertaining to a "half-dead" cashier. If the clerk is dawdling, I might mumble "dream on baby." Or, if she's having a yackety-yak with someone, I might exclaim: "How about getting busy with more work and less socializing!"

At work, I am careful to avoid being totally negligent but it affords me pleasure - waiting until the very last minute - before giving my boss or a co-worker something they had requested.

One afternoon, my supervisor telephoned me at home to request the location of a certain file in my computer. I knew where it was but in a foul mood, I feigned not knowing offhand. With a glow of satisfaction, I kept her waiting for an answer until the following day, at work.

The Gazette had a weekly column called "My Montreal" that invited readers to submit a picture, along with an appropriate notation of what came to mind when they thought of the city. I sent them the photo of a trash can with the comment: "The picture shown here is what comes to mind when thinking of Montreal." It felt pleasure knowing the newspaper columnist and perhaps some of his associates would see my submission depicting Montreal as a garbage receptacle.

I am always intent on hurting the city. There are times, as assistant librarian, I assist college students in researching information. I never fail to advise them, upon graduating and contemplating a career, to relocate out of this urban disaster. I then explain, in some detail, why Montreal is a deplorable city. (See Chapter 9)

The public library has only a few books of the kind I enjoy, mostly narratives of individuals coping with severe illnesses. After having read all they had of that genre, I then spent several frustrating months on a waiting list for a new publication, listed in their catalog. Visits to the library proved fruitless; all the clerks gave me were sharp-tongued excuses, as to why the book was still not available. In a state of sulky dissatisfaction, I began tossing books behind bookshelves, in narrow spaces where the librarians would never think to look; call it my sneaky PAPD payback for their rude, disinterested attitude.

My father recently said: "You now have a more aggressive attitude than ever before!" It was in reference to my destructive wishes for the places I complain about. For example, it galls me that the weekly supermarket flyers only feature mark-downs of junk food, cosmetics and toys. I not only complain that the flyers are a useless waste of paper, but go on to tell him: "I would like to see the printing plant destroyed and the food stores advertising in the flyers get burned to the ground!"

While Father is not privy to my actual passive-aggressive vandalism, he does hear my endless complaints about Montreal, the new millennium and a world that has gone berserk! (See Chapter 34 - The Quickening)

Admittedly, I have fallen into a pattern of dysfunctional living and must release my anger with vandalizing and other PAPD traits. They are the only way of getting through most days without losing what sanity I still have. My grievances are more than justified. If I am to survive in this environment and not throw myself off a bridge, then my passive-aggressive behaviors are an absolute necessity - a temperament of satisfaction I could never relinquish!

People cannot understand why I find it impossible to hold back passive-aggressive urges. The usual psychiatric approach is teaching the client to act-out her frustrations in socially acceptable ways. Actually, I've tried hitting a punching bag and reciting my grievances into a tape recorder. These methods failed miserably; none of my pent-up anger was released. For me, actual vandalism and other PAPD behaviors are the only satisfactions that can alleviate some of life's unfairness. (See Chapter 16 - Behavior Modification)

It is a known fact that people with passive-aggressive tendencies, do more "acting-out" in large, congested, turbulent cities than in small, low-key cities. As a severely autistic woman plagued by Co-morbid neurological disorders, Montreal is the wrong place to live. (See Chapter 21)

I dream of life in a small, laid back city with a gentler pace of life, a hot dry climate, among people who respect the feelings and rights of others; so that much of the PAPD would, in time, begin to fall away.

Many psychiatrists believe that an ongoing life struggle with parents is one reason for PAPD. Though not dismissing the possibility of a biological predisposition, they think that a dysfunctional relationship with one's parents can trigger its development.

Dr. Webster, my current psychiatrist, is exceptionally knowledgeable about the oppositional behaviors presented by clients. He told me that the temperamental mismatches between parents and children present risk factors for the development of oppositional behaviors and adult PAPD traits. He further said, throughout his long career, compared to other patients, he considers my upbringing the *worst mismatch* with parents, he has ever known.

In this new millennium, as I grow increasingly disenchanted with life and world conditions, my rebellious attitude is developing into an outright rejection of the human race.

When I mull over the idea of doing a questionable PAPD behavior, considered disruptive or immoral by others, my attitude is often strong and unyielding. Trying to stop an antisocial behavior from occurring is like trying to hold back a sneeze, or not releasing urine when the bladder is full. (See Chapter 6 - Tourette Syndrome)

CONCLUSION:
Mostly beginning in early adulthood, the essential features of Marla's PAPD are, as follows: vandalism, irritable emotion, behavioral negativity, petty theft, a poor self-image, feeling misunderstood, suicidal thoughts, envy of those more fortunate, feeling luckless in life, verbally aggressive, using manipulative behavior, and scorn for those in authority.

Marla is troubled by a desperate food situation that results in doing frequent vandalism with its motivation best understood in her own words: "When damaging or destroying junk food - for the moment - I do not think of myself as a weak and helpless victim."

As Marla sees it, what follows next is a compilation of threats to our very existence; the planet and humanity perhaps on the brink of annihilation.

34

The Quickening

INTRODUCTION:
In his 1997 book, "The Quickening, Today's Trends, Tomorrow's World," Art Bell pointed out the dangers and new realities we face with today's rapidly changing planet.

Gaining steam in the 1990's and continuing apace in the 21st century, our world is racing into the future with remarkable technological advancements. The ways in which we live, work, play and relate to one another are in flux. For Marla, who thrives on sameness and stability, the ongoing changes feel disruptive and the future seems unnerving.

New technology, world-wide turbulence, terrorism, religious fanaticism, trashing of the earth, emerging diseases and erratic global weather patterns all add to the Quickening. Weapons of mass murder - nuclear, biological and chemical - are proliferating to a degree that our very survival is in jeopardy.

Text:
When we contemplate the 1990's and the new millennium, the Quickening confirms an acceleration of deadly happenings, in a world helpless to do much about them.

I recall the SARS (Severe Acute Respiratory Syndrome) epidemic threat in winter and spring of 2003. Had the plague attacked Montreal, my essential routines would have been ripped apart by a mandatory quarantine lasting two to three weeks!

Soon after, in late July, at the nursing home where I work, a scabies outbreak gave the place a prison-like atmosphere for several days.

In several of the medical journals, published since 1990, I have noticed an increased hopelessness about the future. Announcements of a medical breakthrough, accompanied by extravagant claims, often come to naught; I've become embittered with much of science and medicine.

The interventions doctors advocate are invariably accompanied by unpleasant, even debilitating tradeoffs. For example, cancer treatments designed to prolong the lives of patients are usually accompanied by side effects, ones that impair vitality, cause vomiting, and have unremitting pain. Medical science often moves in reverse as drugs and treatments are withdrawn due to unforeseen side-effects and even death.

Journal articles, based on so-called scientific studies, frequently provide contradictory information with the reader often left in a quandary, not knowing what course of action to take, if any.

As for television, I have a loathing for the incessant advertising and marketing trickery. The consumer gets hoodwinked into buying costly "adult toys" with built-in obsolescence; such things as mega-sized TV's, new model computers, and gas-guzzling SUV's (sports utility vehicles).

The unstable Quickening yields forces that have worsened my neurological disabilities. While autism craves routines of sameness and stability, the Quickening affords me neither and factually gives me just the opposite; I am disgruntled by the accelerating, fast pace of life.

My loathing of a pop-culture hell-bent on more-and-more sex, violence and materialism creates an even greater disconnect between myself and others - far greater than autism per se would have engendered.

The following are Quickening realities that are already occurring or likely to happen in the future:

People factors:
 * Over-population;
 * A non-caring, selfish attitude displayed by individuals and groups;
 * Increased violence, and crime;
 * Undisciplined children and teenagers, out of control;
 * Individuals and gangs who maim and kill for pleasure;
 * An increasingly high divorce rate and lack of family values;
 * More rudeness and lack of respect for others;
 * Genocide or holocaust of mass human slaughter.
 Weather:
 * Global climate change with greater frequency of hurricanes,
   blizzards, ice storms, drought, floods, extreme temperatures,
   tsunamis, and coastal flooding with cities under water.
Health:
 * Inadequate medical care for billions of people;
 * Paucity of social services for those in need;
 * Emergence of deadly new viruses;
 * Increase of bacterial diseases resistant to antibiotics;
 * Strange new sicknesses;
 * Increasing use of illicit, mind-altering drugs;
 * Increased alcoholism;
 * A far greater incidence of overweight and obesity;
 * Mass starvation;
 * Greater abundance of junk food;
 * Healthful, low-calorie foods - often scarce and unaffordable.

Environment:
* Crop failures due to erratic weather conditions;
* Earthquakes;
* Air pollution;
* Water pollution;
* Nuclear waste build-up;
* Solar activity marked by solar flares;
* Volcanoes;
* Forest and brush fires.

Miscellaneous:
* Proliferation of nuclear, chemical and biological weapons;
* New technologies faster than we can assimilate them;
* Wanton global destruction such as deforestation, ozone depletion and the extinction of plant and animal species;
* Growing income inequality, not only between nations but within nations;
* School systems failing to administer quality education:
* No provision made for students' atypical learning styles;
* Buildup of financial debt by individuals and government;
* Monetary inflation;
* Countries lacking adequate water, electric power, sewer systems, roads and means of transportation;
* Most of the world's infrastructure - inadequate or in serious decline.

Climatic global change has caused increased wet weather in Montreal. With the growing number of violent storms, I'm having many more anxiety attacks. During cloudbursts and power outages I agonize with Emotional Meltdowns, and without a soul to "walk me" through any of the crises. With this millennium, more than ever, terribly bad weather and confined to my apartment throws me into a state of Situational Depression. (See Chapters 7 and 35, respectively.)

Quebec separatism*, a political force of the Quickening, is promoted by the French majority in stark conflict with Quebec's English speaking minority. While decades old, the animosity has been heating up since the 1990's. Living in the mainstream of this antagonism and often belittled for not speaking French, I feel like an outsider, no longer a Quebecer, where I was born and have lived all my life. The Separatists are determined to break away from Canada and become an independent country.

Quebec's economic austerity, another offshoot of the Quickening, is eating away at my quality of life. There is a serious lack of social services for disabled people. I have poor hand-eye coordination (Dyspraxia) and desperately require a daily hour of kitchen help, seven days a week. Despite much suffering and great need, all I get is a meager, single hour of help, one day a week! (See Chapter 17)

Prior to the 1990's, there were always a few caring individuals willing to give me a helping hand. In this age of the Quickening, at least in Montreal, people are not supportive; there is neither kindness nor interest in a disabled person's welfare. Among my co-workers and acquaintances, there is zilch psychological or tangible support coming from anyone.

My standard of living keeps dropping with a salary that's been frozen many years; yet there are new taxes, increases in old ones, higher food prices and everything more costly. Canada's inflation continues at a Quickening pace, while my income drops further behind the cost of living.

I have become an embittered rebel of society. Life's losses, due to the Quickening, are super-fueling my passive-aggressive behavior; further pushing me into the hell of *total* dysfunctional living. I've abandoned all of life's frills and fallen into a survivalist mode that has left me interested in nothing except life's simple basics: eating, exercise, sleeping and maintaining my health. Devoid of academic or cultural interests, I lack the desire to do anything useful or productive. With the Quickening misery upon me, I consider any effort beyond a bare existence mode not worth the effort.

During a Quickening emergency, I'd need support from anyone willing to help with my daily routines of outdoor exercise, low calorie food, and home care assistance. A life without these bare necessities would not be worth living.

In the event my lifestyle suffered a temporary interruption, I'd need a physician - to put me under sedation - until my routines could once again normalize. In contrast, the *permanent loss* of my basic lifestyle would give me no choice but to seek the <u>Big S</u>*. (See Chapter 35 – Suicidal Thoughts)

CONCLUSION:
The Quickening is accelerating in a world hell-bent on a proliferation of nuclear, chemical, and biological weapons; many of which are produced by rogue nations in support of terrorism and their reckless determination to obliterate our culture.

These are real issues and the concerns of most thinking people. Yet individuals have the ability to compartmentalize; the insecurities get shunted aside, making it possible to take pleasure in whatever time is left.

Marla is unable to compartmentalize and with fears about the future, she cannot put aside whatever issues of the Quickening might personally affect her. In the meantime, the best she can do is pour out her worries to anyone who will Validate them. (See Chapter 15)

Chapter 35 further discusses Marla's suicidal thoughts.

35

Situational Depression and Suicidal Thoughts

INTRODUCTION:
There is no prescription drug that specifically targets autism. However, antidepressants are routinely prescribed, often with undesirable side effects, to treat symptoms of depression that may accompany autism.

Mental health professionals do not always distinguish between clinical and situational depression. Clinical depression is a psychiatric disorder, characterized by a *long-term* feeling of sadness, the inability to experience pleasure, and a sense of hopelessness. Situational depression is an episode of emotional and psychological depression that occurs in response to a specific set of circumstances, triggered by *environmental factors*.

Marla has never found a medication to be effective for the situational depression that often plagues her; it is a condition that occurs all too frequently when her lifestyle is negatively affected or she perceives a current or impending crisis in her life.

Text:
From time-to-time, Dr. Freedman, my Psychiatrist, had suggested that for my low moods, I should at least try antidepressant prescrip-

tion drugs. Having some familiarity with the literature, I would refuse because of documented side effects. (See Chapter 14)

At the geriatric hospital where I work, co-workers tell me that taking antidepressants would help me feel better. Although I know their advice is well-meant, I am fed up with nurses and others suggesting those drugs as a cure for what ails me.

People need to understand that I *well-know* what is required to not suffer from situational depression, namely: affordable low-calorie food, daily exercise, supportive people, housekeeping services, car rides and a warm climate. I defiantly insist that no pill is going to trick my brain into accepting what, for me, is a wretched Montreal existence. Never will I settle for the artificial feelings of psychiatric drugs and wind-up a "junkie," taking the place of a fulfilled life. With my depression, situational and environmental, antidepressants are not the answer.

Those drugs also deplete the vigor and vitality of one's conscious state, reduce deep thought, and cause sluggishness. For me, somber moods are better tolerated than mind-altering antidepressants.

When under their influence, a patient becomes docile while lacking the all important feelings of being cheerful, happy or optimistic. One feels like an automaton and behaves like one; intent on lying around, eating, smoking, and sleeping - so that weight gain is also a common side effect.

There are also secondary responses such as: insomnia, agitation, tremor and panic attacks; these would negatively affect my ability to function as library assistant, and lose my capacity to hold down a job. Based on the aforementioned side-effects of antidepressants, I much prefer an existence of *untreated*, situational depression.

Admittedly, suicidal feelings creep in when exercise, proper food and <u>tangible support</u>* are missing from my life. A sense of heightened pessimism - about the planet's bleak future - can also trigger a death wish. (See Chapter 34 - The Quickening)

Especially in fall and winter when the inevitable, bad weather keeps me a prisoner indoors, with no exercise possible, <u>pulling the plug</u>* crowds my thinking. In past years, that same impulse occurred whenever a key support person moved away from Montreal.

On top of everything else, the sudden unavailability of a low-calorie food item, important to my meal routine, can dishearten me to the point I have no desire to live.

Now pushing age 50, the thought of dying consoles me because at least I've lived through my teens, twenties and thirties when times were far better. When I mention my loss of interest in living, I mean *this kind* of living; Montreal being the major snag. The thought of being stuck here the rest of my days makes the <u>Big S</u>* an attractive option. If I could return to more normal times, as things were in the 1980's, and live in a decent small city, I could begin enjoying life and stop thinking about death.

A person who abandons life usually stops eating, ceases favorite activities and stays in bed most of the time. Although not obvious in the usual way, people are beginning to notice my disinterest in staying alive. I'm reacting with considerable passive aggressive behavior and refuse any involvement in constructive pursuits. My life has become one of bare existence, hanging on by a thread!

Never once acting on it, co-workers who have known me for a long time, do not take my suicidal talk seriously. In contrast, a few others who hardly knew me, reported my death wish to their supervisor; she in turn alerted our health care nurse. When called to her office, I discussed my unhappiness, and she was supportive. It was during the time I worked in Housekeeping as a charwoman - a job I hated and had frequent death wishes!

Then shortly later, being assigned to tryout for a job in the library, Mother surmised that the health nurse in tandem with the union prevailed upon the administration to create the new position. (See Chapter 26 - Medical Library Assistant)

People are sometimes disturbed by my suicidal moods and although such thoughts have been more frequent in recent months, my wish to die is not constant. If I ever had a disease like cancer, multiple sclerosis or an injury that left me paralyzed, I'd absolutely and positively want to end it all. But, in the world's current state of what I consider a *dysfunctional millennium,* I do "threaten myself" with suicide but have yet to attempt it.

The only other event causing me to contemplate death is my father's passing; an event that would leave me with no support and unable to survive.

CONCLUSION:
Since Marla's depression is situational, it makes sense that she desires to significantly *change* her situation and not attempt to camouflage environmental problems with brain-numbing anti-depressants.

Whenever overly troubled by life's problems, Marla ponders suicide. So far, it has been an idle threat but one that has worsened in both frequency and intensity during this millennium. It cannot be taken lightly and she deserves ongoing verbal and material support, so that suicide is no longer an option.

NOTE

High-functioning autism (HFA) is sometimes referred to as <u>Asperger syndrome</u>*. Regarding an essay entitled: *Asperger's Syndrome - Behaviour Issues: A Psychological Approach*, by *Dr. Amitta Shah, UK, 1999*, Dr. Shah's paper addresses the psychological difficulties endured by adults with high-functioning autism.

Consistent with Dr. Shah's philosophy, instead of Marla drugging herself with anti-depressant medications, the Shah approach would be a change of environment; one that would allow Marla's unfulfilled needs to be rekindled. It is reasonable to assume that in the new locale her situational depression would be infrequent and she'd no longer have a death wish.

The next chapter deals with the untimely loss of Marla's mother.

36

Mother's Death

Tragedy:
Early one winter morning, Marla's mother went downstairs into the basement and lit a match. Her nightgown was ignited by a spark and burst into flames; she suffered severe burns over most of her body.

Mr. Comm summoned help.

Rushed to the hospital, she lived for eleven days, but died of third degree burns, on January 28, 2000, at age 69.

The loss and shock felt by Marla was expressed in a short memorial poem, written by her, appearing in the Montreal Gazette death notice section.

Marla's poem follows:

Dedicated to Millie Comm
You were a kind and loving wife,
A mother and a friend.
Sad was I the day your life
Came to such a sudden end.

You were always filled with hope,
Words of cheer and praise.
You always found the strength to cope
Even in the darkest days.

I will miss our morning walks
In the mountain air,
And the long and thoughtful talks
That we had up there.

I remember wistfully,
As I sit here dressed in black
The mother that you were to me
And only wish that you'd come back.

By Marla Comm

Text:
Because of the poem, I received abundant praise from family members and hospital co-workers. Basking in this recognition gave me considerable pleasure.

There was an outpouring of shock and grief by staff people who had known Mother during the years she worked at Maimonides Geriatric Centre as a secretary prior to retirement, and where I still work as assistant medical librarian. Being her daughter, I was the recipient of warm emotion from people who remembered her.

As for funeral preparations, I lacked Executive Function ability needed to help with the arrangements. In my own mind this feeling of inadequacy counteracted the recognition and praise I had received for writing the poem. (See Chapter 20)

In contrast to how Father must have felt disappointed with me, my sister Sherry was praised to the sky for assisting with funeral arrangements, handling the many phone calls, and doing much of the paperwork.

Knowing my dislike of social affairs, especially funerals, my father knew there was no way I could endure several full days of sitting Shiva*. He spoke with Dr. Freedman who suggested that I not be duty-bound to participate entire days and evenings. Father agreed and I only had to attend services a few hours each afternoon.

If fate had it that Father was the one who died and had it been Mother's decision, my psychiatrist's suggestion would have fallen on deaf ears; she would have insisted on my full Shiva attendance all seven days!

Co-workers who in the past had ignored me or treated me like dirt suddenly became warm and caring. A woman working in the finance department, with whom I never got along, became a different person toward me. One day seeing me with teary eyes, she called me into her office and said she'd be available to help me with a problem whenever Christine, my usual support person, was busy. In addition, she offered to give me car rides on weekends whenever she had the time.

It was no more than a few weeks after the funeral, she flipped back to her normal, cold fish persona; all the previous sympathy, caring and promises were quickly forgotten!

There was new found support by JFS* in pledging more rides to the mountain. Peter* and my social worker also gave assurances they would do all they could to get me the household services I needed. (See Chapter 13 - Four Letdowns)

Their promises were soon forgotten, as was the case with my hospital co-workers. With no follow-through of any kind by anyone, it was soon "back to business as usual."

Mother's demise taught me an important lesson. The sudden caring and outpouring of support were nothing more than social convention - playacting of short duration - brought on by an untimely death.

I was naive getting my hopes up, believing there were now co-workers and others willing to provide occasional psychological and tangible support. In retrospect, I wish nobody had ever come near me with their saccharine condolences because the way it turned out, I felt more rejected than ever.

Having autism, it was with much nervous tension that I went along with their insincere social game. It required several days of *forced sociality*, all the while feeling as though my innards were being torn apart! Admittedly, it was behavior totally at odds with my true personality, one that harbors a general dislike of humanity. My insincere, false behavior was mainly to gain praise from others and have them consider me a loving daughter; it was designed to receive their future verbal and tangible support, when needed.

I concede that *heartfelt love* was not my prime motive for writing the poem; rather it was to reinforce promises made by co-workers for their support. In retrospect, all of us, each in our own way, were being deceptive or, at the very least, insincere.

CONCLUSION:
Now with Mother gone and Father, in his senior years, the only support person in her life, Marla worries about the future.

The next chapter advocates for the rights of autistic adults.

37

An Individual's Rights

NOTE:
One of this book's underpinnings is to advocate improvements for Marla and countless other autistic people, living in the mainstream, who suffer from dysfunctional lives. The preponderance of individuals, with neurological disorders, *require ongoing supportive counseling* from a psychiatrist, psychologist or a qualified social worker.

It should be emphasized, when a <u>spectrum</u>* individual reaches maturity, no therapist has an ethical or legal right to dictate the patient's lifestyle. Methodology must always be tailored to the legitimatefelt needs of each client.

In North America there is a general policy, among mental health professionals, to terminate treatment sessions with clients who are unable or unwilling to *improve*, according to the therapist's beliefs and standards.

In most locales, counseling is only provided, when the client agrees to make *changes* in their personality, by accepting a type of behavior modification and/or a willingness to use psychiatric drugs. Using persuasive power, convincing a client to follow such a course, is a violation of his civil rights.

Therapists must no longer deny autistic individuals regularly, scheduled counseling treatment. These sessions are needed to discuss all manner of the patient's problems - if he/she is to have a functional personal life, hold down a job, have constructive diversions, and "survive" in the real world.

It is appropriate for the mental health professional to apprise the client of any special treatment options, deemed worthwhile, but actual acceptance must always be the client's prerogative.

In this millennium, mental health professionals have a tendency to think in lockstep when it comes to treatment. In essence, clients are often prodded to change their personality through behavior modification and develop, what the culture deems, socially acceptable traits. This approach fails taking into account the inflexibility of autism and its synergy with other inflexible neurological disorders.

For the many individuals whose neuro-hardwiring* is incapable of variation, no type of behavior modification should be insisted upon. On the other hand, it should be available for those who want it and feel they can endure the rigors of change. If the patient, at some point, is no longer desirous of continuing the program, it should be discontinued.

While dysfunctional moods are stressful, Marla finds them more tolerable than prescription drug side effects. Antidepressants were tried in the past, converting her into a docile couch potato. Again it is worth emphasizing that pressuring clients to use prescription drugs is a violation of their civil rights. (See Chapter 14 - Psychiatrist and Medications)

Other than being a good listener, the role of the therapist is to be supportive, while sharing an exchange of thoughts, feelings, new perspectives and insights with the client.

CONCLUSION:

Despite the heavy taxation that pays for Canada's socialized medicine, Marla and others, like her, are shortchanged by the system's violation of human rights. Unless, they agree to psychiatric drugs and/or types of behavior modification, they are *denied* psychotherapy. These are countless, mainstream autistic adults, with multiple neurological disorders, who are *denied supportive services*; many of whom then become the nation's invisible throwaways.

Especially, for those involved in the life of an autistic person, the final chapter is a compilation of mistakes to be avoided.

38

A Summing Up
Mistakes and Lost Opportunities

Note:
Marla was an atypical child with multiple brain disorders. Had she been treated with kindness, understanding and sophistication her adult life adjustment would now be far better.

In early childhood, she was often left in a play pen for hours at a time, while her mother did typing at home to earn extra family income. Though Marla did not object to the solitude, it was a routine that may have reinforced her disinterest in human contact. In any event, those long periods left alone were *Mistake Number One*.

(Infants and toddlers need the touching and cuddling of bodily stimulation; not receiving it can engender neurological disorders and worsen existing ones. Marla's autistic lack of sociality rejected any close human contact, depriving her of physical stimulation needed for normal brain development.)

The parents should have tried a <u>workaround</u>* strategy by attempting physical contact in small doses; all the while taking cues from Marla as to what she could tolerate at any given time. As the infant became used to it, there's a good chance she would have accepted more-and-more parental stimulation.

Mr. and Mrs. Comm's concern was solely about their daughter's speech problem, because at age 3 and 3 months she had no speaking ability. She was taken to a neurological clinic for evaluation by Dr. Hunt, a child psychiatrist and his staff. In addition to lack of speech, a marked aloofness toward the doctor and his assistant was observed. With lack of speech and social coldness, Marla was diagnosed with autism as noted in the clinic records, but her parents were never given this vital information.

In a few months she began speaking and a return visit was made to the clinic. Mr. Comm lauded the fact that his daughter now had speech ability and even developed a *liking for people*. While Marla was now able to speak, the psychiatrist noted in her chart that he saw no evidence of improved sociality.

The parents believed that her only dysfunction was lack of speech and now that she was talking, they were quite satisfied. As very private people, they never felt comfortable with the staff's questioning. Mr. Comm made it clear that except for a future pre-kindergarten evaluation, he saw no further need for visits to the clinic. (*Mistake Number Two*)

Marla's so-called liking for people was pure fiction; she remained aloof as ever, and both parents reacted in kind - giving her no physical stimulation. (*Mistake Number Three*)

At age 5, Mrs. Comm had Marla evaluated by the clinic to find out if kindergarten would be a good idea. Dr. Hunt said that he was in favor of a kindergarten experience, but it was important that the teacher be made aware of Marla's problematic aloofness. Ignoring Dr. Hunt's advice, they made no special contact with the teacher. (*Mistake Number Four*)

Mistake Number Five was Dr. Hunt not advising the parents that their daughter, due to autism, should be sent to a private school with a small class register and given special education. Instead, she was enrolled in public kindergarten with its large register and taunted by the other children.

As schooling progressed, Marla's autism prevented normal cognitive development. She had trouble comprehending people subjects like history and literature; fiction books with human stories made no sense to her. By not substituting some understandable non-fiction books, every teacher did Marla a disservice, perhaps unknowingly. (*Mistake Number Six*)

Throughout twelve years of public education, Marla was often in conflict with classmates and mostly ignored by teachers. Since she had high intelligence, what might have been an enriched education in private school was instead a virtual waste of time in public school.

In the way Marla was raised, both parents were in denial that anything was *seriously* wrong with her; call this: (*Mistake Number Seven*).

They were sure that her poor sociality, negativism, <u>tics</u>* and other atypical behaviors would be outgrown, helped along by their rules and strict discipline. (*Mistake Number Eight*)

Parental hollering and verbal abuse made matters worse; Marla rebelled and became even more set in her negative ways. Despite using harsh methods which failed, they blindly continued along the same path. (*Mistake Number Nine*)

At age 14, she began seeing Dr. Freedman, a child psychiatrist and autism specialist. During his weekly counseling, he was most supportive and never attempted to force any treatment on Marla that she opposed. In therapy, Marla talked about her run-ins with people and difficulties caused by multiple, neurological disorders. While the doctor gave credence to Marla's autism, he downplayed her Dyspraxia and SID; he considered them minor traits although she made it known they created more aggravation in her life than autism! (See Chapters 17 and 18, respectively.)

While she was still young enough to perhaps benefit from <u>OT</u>* treatment, for Dyspraxia and SID, he neither made the referral nor suggested that her parents do it. (*Mistake Number Ten*)

Throughout therapy, Dr. Freedman had periodic meetings with Mr. and Mrs. Comm. By the time Marla became a young adult, had a job and lived in her own apartment, he suggested that Mom and Dad feel free to travel at will; he said Marla would be able to manage on her own. Dr. Freedman seriously erred by discounting Marla's need for daily verbal support plus the occasional car ride. To fill these needs while her parents were out of town, he did not think it necessary that she receive backup support from a relative or family friend. (*Mistake Number Eleven*)

When Marla began working, Dr. Freedman put a great deal of emphasis on her employment and gave little attention to her personal life. He believed that if she could continue holding down a job, do self care and feed herself, she was doing just fine and did not require the support of others. (*Mistake Number Twelve*)

Because of SID and dyspraxia, doing Kitchen chores have always been an ordeal for Marla, resulting in smashed kitchens and chewed-up arms. Paid for by CLSC, the only help she receives is a single hour, one day a week. As for the other six days, she gets zilch help from CLSC; the result is an evening supper routine, ongoing in sheer chaos! (*Mistake Number Thirteen*) (See Chapter 11)

If the insufficient homecare was due to CLSC austerity, Marla's social worker might have solicited this important help from a local charity, foundation or other resource, but she has never been willing to put forth the effort. (*Mistake Number Fourteen*)

A preponderance of mental health professionals have a hard and fast rule that any psychotherapy should be based on the patient's willingness to improve his/her lifestyle with methods such as <u>occupational therapy</u>*, physiotherapy, psychotropic drugs and behavior modification. When therapists engage *solely* in supportive counseling, the establishment considers it an improper use of mental health resources. (*Mistake Number Fifteen*)

For someone like Marla, living on the edge, with neither the desire nor fortitude for change, it is poor judgment to insist on lifestyle *modifications* as a condition to receive psychotherapy. To his credit, Dr. Freedman accepted Marla's need for supportive counseling and while he occasionally made suggestions for change, they were never forced on her.

Since Dr. Freedman's death, Marla began seeing another psychiatrist, the only one who had an opening. While he is forever attempting to force change on her, she consistently shoots it down. By not providing the supportive counseling Marla craves, the sessions are mostly wasted (*Mistake Number Sixteen*)

Two psychotherapists come to mind who believe in counseling patients based on their special needs; not a one-size-fits-all dictatorial policy, handed down by a governmental agency or a clique of mental health professionals, these therapists are:

<u>Dr. Christopher Gillberg</u>*, in the UK, is a psychiatrist whose lifelong career has been devoted to autism research and treatment. In his book, "A *Guide to <u>Asperger Syndrome</u>*,*" he explains that despite some key similarities, those with high functioning autism are all quite different; so that his respect for the special needs of each individual takes precedence over all else.

<u>Dr. Amitta Shah</u>*, also in the UK, has a similar philosophy. In her essay, "*Asperger's Syndrome - Behavior Issues: A Psychological Approach,*" she says that when treating an individual, she focuses on *underlying causes*, different for each client. Besides her supportive therapy, she counsels patients in ways to improve their coping strategies and increase their tolerance toward others.

CONCLUSION:
For parents, mental health professionals, educators and others who interact with neurologically challenged individuals, it is our wish they can avoid the kinds of mistakes that have devastated Marla's life; perhaps gleaned from the book and this last chapter.

Millennium

Hidden in the depths of time
And space a mighty power lay;
It watched us for 2000 years
And came one special New Year's Day.

In the middle of the night
That New Year's Eve it struck,
Ringing in an era filled
With sickness, hardship and bad luck.

It tore a path of devastation
As it crept from town to town,
Bringing mayhem to the streets,
And burning buildings down.

It promised even deeper grief
To those already sad.
It stalked the poor and took away
What little they still had.

It gathered storm clouds in the sky,
Compelled the wind to blow,
Drenched the world with pounding rain
And smothered it with snow.

It pierced the sky with lightning bolts,
Scorched the earth with searing heat,
Then plunged it into deep freeze
And pummeled it with sleet.

It turned the fields that once sustained us
Into barren waste
And brought us famines even worse
Than any we have ever faced.

It spewed out smoke and poison vapors,
Tainted all the seas,
Spread pestilence and sickened us
With strange and deadly maladies.

It filled our minds with evil thoughts,
Our hearts with greed and lust,
Turned kindness into hatred
And faith into mistrust.

It set us all against each other,
Filled us all with spite,
Divided friends and families,
Inspired us to fight.

It overwhelmed our spirits
With a tense malaise
That drove us into whirlwind lives
Of sleepless nights and frenzied days.

It wooed us into foolish pastimes,
Vain and worthless enterprise,
And led us into wayward lives
Founded on pretense and lies.

It gave us the bravado
And daring to explore
The murky and forbidden realms
We dared not venture near before.

It taught us how to build machines
That held us spellbound and in awe
But that brought us face to face
With dangers none of us foresaw.

It led to dark discoveries,
Grim and bitter truths laid bare,
Realities that shattered hopes
And threw us deep into despair.

It terrorized us for a year,
Taking out its wrath
On those of us unfortunate
Enough to step into its path.

On and on it rages
And with each passing year
Grows even fiercer as it feeds
Off our anguish and our fear.

The world knew it was coming
Since antiquity.
It was mankind's future,
And his final destiny.

Many feared and dreaded it,
Yet they still held on,
To the hope that when it came
A golden age of light would dawn.

We, the ones who greeted it,
Recall what those before us said
And with great regret admit
That darkness fell instead.

---Written by Marla Comm

Shattered Dreams

Many, many years ago
Some daring souls set forth
For unknown lands and stumbled on
This rugged country in the north.

The rough and windswept wilderness
They ventured to explore
In hopes that it would lead them to
The riches they were looking for.

They sailed on and found an island
And through years of toil
Built themselves a village
On its frozen soil.

Many followed in the footsteps
Of those daring men
And crossed the very ocean
Those voyagers did way back when.

Some sailed down the river
That took them to the weatherworn
Island where a tiny village
Centuries ago was born.

They braved the cold and ploughed their way
Through the ice and snow
Tilled the land and laid down roots
And prayed that they'd begin to grow.

At first they throve and prospered
But then the hard times came
The city that was once their pride
Would one day hang its head in shame.

The long and bitter winters
Were more than they could bear
The hatred and oppression
Drove them to despair.

More and more they longed for peace
And hungered for the sun
And those blessed with good fortune
Fled the city one by one.

Some headed south; some headed west
To start their lives anew
And with the past behind them
Prospered once again and grew.

While the hapless souls they left
Behind them sadly had to stay
In the frozen waste and watch
Their lives just slowly slip away.

Those have-nots stranded on the island
Shorn of hope and penniless
Knew they had no future
In the frozen wilderness.

They simmered with resentment
They quarreled and they fought
And let the city many labored
Hard to build and nurture rot.

Weary and disheartened
They can only sit
And watch with resignation
As it crumbles bit by bit.

In their disappointment
They reflect on days gone by
When the great explorers
Stepped ashore with hopes held high.

And the dreams that drove those men
To push their luck and roam
A vast and yet uncharted land
And make that land their home.

Then they humbly tell themselves
As they battle wind and rain
And fester in the filth and squalor
That those dreams were all in vain.

And lament their own dashed hopes
The freedom and prosperity
That they once envisioned
And now know they'll never see.

Stranded on that wretched island
On whose frozen, storm-tossed land
The weather-beaten ruins
They humbly call their city stand.

--Written by Marla Comm

My True Home

The desert sun is beckoning,
Calling me away
To a land where balmy breezes
Blow and palm trees sway.

A land far from this blighted island
City where I spent
More than forty years
Languishing in discontent.

Here is where my roots are;
No other place I know,
But my heart lies elsewhere,
Far from all the ice and snow.

Through bleak and sunless days I sit
Dreaming of a far off land
Where centuries old saguaros rise
From the sun-baked desert sand.

I dream of an idyllic place
Where I can frolic in the sun,
Where time stands still and all the days
Melt together into one.

And where I can ride through town,
In the gentle morning breeze
As it bathes me with the soothing,
Smoky scent of mesquite trees.

I dream of open air fiestas
Pulsing with the salsa beat
And alive with carefree people
Dancing in the street.

I always had that feeling;
I always knew deep down
That my true home lay miles away
In some southern desert town.

I was never happy here;
I never felt at home
In this wretched city
Where savages and paupers roam.

I grew to dread the endless winters,
Diving rains and biting chill,
The snowdrifts and the sound of sleet
Banging on my window sill.

I'm weary of the whiny rock songs,
Stale smoke and cheap perfume,
Greasy fries and squalor,
And heavy gray November gloom.

This city is a wasteland,
A sick and troubled place that teems
With frenzied mobs that fill the air
With angry honks and piercing screams.

Its people speak a language
Different from my own;
I was born and raised here
But feel unwelcome and alone.

I look beyond the neon lights,
The bustle and the frills and see
The damp and dreary wilderness
I know this place to really be.

Every time I watch the raindrops
Falling from the clouds above,
I tell myself this is a place
That I will never grow to love.

If only I could break away,
Start all over and set forth
For a peaceful desert town
Far from this prison in the north.

Here I'll only fade away
And suffocate in my despair;
I know where my true home lies
And wish someone could take me there.

---**Written by Marla Comm**

GLOSSARY

A

Asperger syndrome: A pervasive developmental disorder, on the autism spectrum and not a mental illness. It is synonymous with high-functioning autism (HFA), but without a clinically significant language delay.

Assisted living: A supportive housing facility or group home, designed for those who need extra help in their day-to-day lives.

Aura: A bright light that precedes the onset of a migraine headache attack.

B

Big S: Slang for suicide..

Burnout: Physical and emotional problems that often result from excessive pressure in the workplace. Symptoms include physical and emotional exhaustion.

C

Cabin fever: A condition of restlessness and irritability, caused by spending too much time indoors..

CLSC - Centre Locale de Services Communautaires: Quebec's Community Social Services

CNS - Central nervous system: consisting of the brain and spinal cord.

D

Denial: An unconscious, psychological defense mechanism, characterized by refusal to acknowledge painful realities..

Developmentally disabled: Disabilities inborn or beginning early in childhood.

F

Fine motor: Skills that refer to coordinating small movements of hands, wrists, fingers and other small muscles of the body.

Flame: Computer Slang. an act or instance of angry criticism or disparagement, esp. on a computer network.

G

Gillberg, Christopher (MD): World renowned authority in the field of autism spectrum disorders.

Good Samaritan: A person who voluntarily offers tangible help or verbal support in times of need.

Grandin, Temple (PhD): Highly accomplished and well-known adult with high functioning autism.

Gross motor: The use of big muscles in the body including legs, arms and abdomen.

Group home: (See Assisted living)

H

Hardwired: Neurological mechanisms; made automatic or inborn - and not modifiable.

HFA - High-Functioning Autism: An individual with autism, having an IQ in the normal range or above.

J

Jesus cult: A religious organization and its system of religious worship.

JFS - Jewish Family Services:. A charitable organization that offers a variety of services, designed to support and help individuals in the Montreal Jewish community.

L

Linear thinking: A thought process that follows a step-by-step progression, where a response to a step must be elicited before another step is taken.

Linda: A sibling, seven years younger than Marla. Linda was diagnosed with cancer at age 15, and succumbed a few months after her 19th birthday.

List group: A joining of people on the Internet, for holding group discussions on topics of special interest and using e-mail.

M

Mainstream: Represents the prevalent attitudes, values, and practices of a society or group

Material support: Support that is real or concrete, as opposed to verbal support consisting of words..

Mt. Royal: A mountain on the island of Montreal, used by Marla for walking the trail.

N

Neuro-disorders: Abnormalities having to do with the nerves or nervous system.

Neuro-hardwiring: Brain mechanisms automatic or inborn.

Neuro-psychiatric: Relating to a mental disorder.

NT - Neurotypical:. A term used to describe a person whose neurological development and state of mind are typical - conforming to what most people perceive as normal.

O
OT - Occupational Therapy:. A procedure done by a trained therapist; who evaluates and may treat an individual with a disorder or impairment that interferes with daily functioning.

P
Persona: One's public image or personality, as distinguished from the inner self.

Peter: Peter Zwack (See Chapter 13)

Psychogenic: Originating in the mind, rather than physiological in origin.

Psychological support: Verbal support as opposed to tangible or material support.

Pulling the plug: Slang expression of opting for sucicide.

Q
Quebec separatism: A political movement for the attainment of sovereignty in Quebec and exercise their right of self-determination.

S
Schizoid personality: A psychiatric condition characterized by a lifelong pattern of indifference to others and a desire for social isolation.

Shah, Amitta (PhD): A United Kingdom authority in the field of autism spectrum disorders.

Sherry: Marla's NT sibling who is a year younger.

Sitting Shiva: In Judaism, a formal seven-day period of mourning the death of a close relative that is observed after the funeral .

Situational depression: An episode of emotional and psychological depression that is not lifelong but occurs in response to a specific set of circumstances.

Skill set: A group of skills needed to do most anything, i.e. tasks and activities.

Snowbird: A person who moves from a cold place to a warm place for the winter.

Spectrum people: Those having any variation of autism.

SSRI: A class of antidepressant drugs.

Sternberg, Dr. Robert J: Proposes the concept of "practical intelligence;" finding the best fit between oneself and the environment.

Stressor: Internal or external factor or stimuli that produces stress.

Support network: Two or more people providing tangible and/or psychological support.

Synergy: The interaction of two or more neurological disorders, so that their combined effect is greater than the sum total of their individual effects.

T
Tangible support: Material support as opposed to verbal support.

Tics: Repetitive, stereotyped movements or vocalizations, such as blinking, sniffing, touching the ground, or tensing the abdomen.

TS - Tourette Syndrome: A neurological disorder that typically appears in childhood. The main features of TS are repeated movements and vocalizations called tics. TS can also be associated with behavioral and developmental problems.

V

Voice inflection: Alteration in pitch or tone of the voice.

W

Website: A connected group of pages on the World Wide Web regarded as a single entity, usually maintained by one person and devoted to one or more related topics.

Window of opportunity: A relatively short period of time during which an opportunity must be acted on, or missed.

Workaround: A method temporarily used for achieving a task or goal when the usual method is not working or is unavailable.

ISBN 142511621-3

9 781425 116217